A Shell Guide

Leicestershire

The west end of STAPLEFORD church

A Shell Guide

Leicestershire

by W G Hoskins

London: Faber & Faber

First published in 1970
by Faber and Faber Limited
24 Russell Square London WC1
Printed in Great Britain by
Billing & Sons Limited
Guildford and London
All rights reserved
ISBN 0 571 09467 8

While the author is here expressing his personal views, Shell-Mex and BP are pleased to be associated with his book

To J. H.
Whose domestic skill enables
the author to live and work
in Victorian comfort

Illustrations

Front endpaper
Gargoyles:
Tilton
Christopher Dalton
Hallaton
John Piper

Frontispiece
Stapleford church
A. E. M. Hartley

Title page
Kings Norton church
Edwin Smith

Page
7 Garendon
John Piper

8 Croxton Kerrial
Christopher Dalton

8 Bringhurst near Nevill Holt
John Piper

10–11 From Burrough-on-the-Hill
John Piper

12 Tilton
Christopher Dalton

13 Coston, gargoyle
John Piper

13 Gargoyles at Lowesby
John Piper

14 Ulverscroft Priory
Peter Burton

15 Charnwood Forest
Peter Burton

17 Grand Union Canal nr.
Laughton
Barnaby's Picture Library

17 Grand Union Canal nr.
Smeeton Westerby
Edward Piper

18 Breedon-on-the-Hill
Peter Burton

18 Belvoir
Peter Burton

18 Saltby
Christopher Dalton

20 Knighton
Christopher Dalton

20 Kirby Bellars
John Piper

21 Queniborough
Peter Burton

24 Appleby Magna
Peter Burton

Page
25 Appleby Parva
Peter Burton

27 Ashby-de-la-Zouch castle
Peter Burton

29 Belvoir castle
Peter Burton

30 Tomb in Bottesford church
A. E. M. Hartley

31 Tomb in Bottesford church
Peter Burton

34 Frieze at Breedon-on-the-
Hill, detail
Peter Burton

35 Bringhurst churchyard
John Piper

36 Squires tomb, Burton Lazars
Peter Burton

37 Ramparts on Burrough-on-
the-Hill
Peter Burton

39 Cold Overton manor
Peter Burton

41 Cold Overton
Christopher Dalton

42 Coston
John Piper

43 Coston, stained glass
John Piper

44 Edmondthorpe, Smith tomb
Peter Burton

47 Foxton Locks
Peter Burton

49 Gaddesby church, south aisle
John Piper

50 Gaddesby
John Piper

51 Gaddesby, medieval benches
John Piper

51 Gaddesby, the Cheney
monument
John Piper

53 Galby
John Piper

55 Great Dalby
John Piper

56 Hallaton, detail of tower
John Piper

57 Hallaton
Peter Burton

Page
58 Houghton-on-the-Hill
F. L. Attenborough

59 Kegworth:
Peter Burton

60 Kings Norton church
Christopher Dalton

61 Kings Norton
John Piper

62 Kegworth workshop
F. L. Attenborough

63 Kirby Muxloe castle
John Piper

64 Leicester, castle gatehouse
Christopher Dalton

65 Leicester, The Crescent
Christopher Dalton

67 Leicester Cathedral, slate
tomb
Edwin Smith

68 Leicester Cathedral, interior
Edwin Smith

69 Leicester, St. Mary de Castro
Christopher Dalton

70 Leicester; The White House
Edwin Smith

71 Leicester University,
Engineering Building
The Architectural Review

72 Little Stretton church
Christopher Dalton

74 The Royal Arms at
Lockington
John Piper

75 The Royal Arms at Kegworth
Christopher Dalton

77 Lubenham
Peter Burton

78 Market Harborough, inn sign
Edwin Smith

79 Market Harborough, spire
Peter Burton

80 Melton Mowbray
Peter Burton

82 Melton Mowbray,
Nottingham St.,
Barnaby's Picture Library

83 Melton Mowbray: derelict
station
Rigby Graham

5

84 Mountsorrel
Peter Burton

85 Narborough, slate headstone
John Piper

86 Nevill Holt
John Piper

89 Noseley, woodcarving
Christopher Dalton

90 Prestwold
A. F. Kersting

92 Saxby
Christopher Dalton

93 Shearsby
Christopher Dalton

94 South Croxton, font
John Piper

95 South Croxton church
Christopher Dalton

96 Sproxton
John Piper

97 Stapleford, tomb
John Piper

98 Stapleford
John Piper

100 Staunton Harold, church interior
Peter Burton

101 Staunton Harold gate
John Piper

102 Stockerston Hall
Peter Burton

103 Stoke Golding
Peter Burton

104 Stonesby
John Piper

105 Swithland churchyard
John Piper

107 Twycross
Peter Burton

108 Near Ulverscroft, cottage
Peter Burton

111 Waltham-on-the-Wolds
F. L. Attenborough

112 Wigston Magna, field pattern
J. Allan Cash

113 Wistow Hall
Christopher Dalton

114 Wistow
John Piper

115 Wistow
John Piper

116 Withcote church, interior
John Piper

116 Withcote church
Peter Burton

117 Withcote, stained glass
Peter Burton

118 Withcote Hall
Peter Burton

Back endpaper
Staunton Harold church, ironwork
Peter Burton

Acknowledgements

I am grateful to the staff of the county record office at Leicester for answering my many enquiries while this book was being written, and to my former and perfect secretary, Mrs Muriel Phillips, for typing my manuscript amid many other duties. And to Mr Jack Brownlow of Melton Mowbray for much help with the history and buildings of that unique town out of his vast and detailed knowledge. All authors' wives are long-suffering: my own wife is, I hope, suitably thanked (with masculine egotism) in the dedication and, by implication, in the Introduction.

GARENDON: relics in the park

Introduction

All counties suffer from popular myths about them—that Staffordshire, for example, is nothing but the Black Country with the Potteries thrown in for good measure; that Devon is red and smiling everywhere; that Essex is one congealed mass of commuters. So Leicestershire is generally dismissed by those who have merely driven through it on the A.6 as flat, pretty well covered with red-brick towns and villages, with somewhere in the unseen background a lot of fox-hunting going on.

I lived in Leicestershire for a good number of years and came to regard the eastern half of the county as some of the most appealing scenery in the whole of England: rolling green hills, valleys dotted with little ironstone churches shining in the afternoon sun, Jacobean and Georgian country houses in remote parks, all of it lovely at any time of the year; on the whole a huge empty countryside with sign-posts pointing along by-roads to villages that were deserted centuries ago. The western side of the county I never came to like, though I am frequently told this merely shows a lack of such a detailed knowledge as I have of the east.

Leicestershire is one of the smaller counties, part of the East Midlands. It is sharply divided, as I have just said, between east and west, the dividing line being the valley of the Soar, one of the lesser rivers of England, which runs roughly due north to join the Trent, through a valley that for miles is fog-bound in autumn and flooded with cold, muddy waters in winter. Much of it is totally unattractive at any time of the year, a kind of half-derelict scruffy edge to the conurbation of Leicester, with some of the dreariest villages one could hope to see anywhere in Britain. There is something unbeatable about industrial red brick put up in the decades be-

tween about 1880 and 1910. Even John Betjeman's heart would shrink at most of it, though there are moments of memorable ugliness suddenly encountered that redeem the general boredom.

But enough of this. The two halves of the county are, as I say, sharply divided between east and west. The boundary is not quite the river-valley, as Leicester has spread a little towards the east; but within five or six miles of leaving the centre of the city one enters perfect country. Indeed, there is one way out of Leicester that takes one from a Victorian suburb into green pastures within a mile or two.

This, too, makes the city of Leicester sound like something to escape from as quickly as possible. It is certainly not. It is one of the oldest towns in England, and behind the rather commonplace impression it makes at first sight it has managed to retain outstanding monuments of almost every age of English history. Nor is it just the charm of antiquity: some of the mid- and late-Victorian parts of the town, the opulent middle-class purlieus of the years between 1860 and 1914, with their wide, tree-shaded roads, have a deeply appealing atmosphere about them, above all on those long melancholy April evenings and perhaps, too, on sunny October mornings when the Midland wind blows briskly along the residential roads, speaking of winter and the lecture season for the serious-minded.

East Leicestershire—often called "High Leicestershire"—runs up to and over the marl-stone escarpment, part of the great Stone Belt that crosses England from the Dorset to the Yorkshire coast. In Leicestershire the limestone that makes up most of this Belt has given way to the golden ironstone or marlstone, no less

attractive than the oolitic limestone of the Cotswolds though by no means so good a building stone. Indeed, wherever it was used in churches and houses, it had to be reinforced at the edges, so to speak, in quoins, window-frames, and so on, by the harder limestone. But because it crumbles so readily, becomes so easily weather-beaten, the old village churches have nearly always an air of pleasing Arnoldian decay. Melancholy on a grey winter day, shining like old gold on a summer evening, they are always a pleasure to look at. This stone lasts long enough: in scores of places it is seven hundred or more years old and still stands up to the Midland weather. A worry to churchwardens and parsons, no doubt, but so deeply appealing, so redolent of ancient worship in a way that the harder stones never can quite achieve. I think especially of South Croxton and Tilton at any time of the year; but east Leicestershire is full of these treasures, often with a 17th-century manor house hard by to complete the utter Englishness of the country scene.

Much of High Leicestershire is over 600 feet up. The highest point is Whatborough Hill (755 ft. above the grey North Sea) where the wind, so they proudly say in the East Midlands, blows straight from the Siberian wastes, with a "lost village" on its very summit. No wonder the early village of Whatborough disappeared from that windswept plateau so long ago—back in Henry VII's time, and decaying long before that.

West Leicestershire has its own uplands in Charnwood Forest. It is only a forest in the technical (that is, legal) sense: a piece of country that was set aside for hunting game as far back as the 12th century. It was, of course, wooded in the ordinary sense too, but not a continuous forest—woods, large clearings and rock-strewn valleys made up a typical hunting country of a different kind from the sweeping grasslands of

TILTON

ULVERSCROFT Priory

Georgian and Victorian generations. The ancient pre-Cambrian rocks of Charnwood rise to over 800 ft. in a few places, and to their highest point in Bardon Hill (912 ft.). Formerly it was a huge wilderness, but the enclosure of 1829 tamed it in places, driving more roads, and straight Roman-like roads, across the wastes. In recent years the M.1 has driven through it in a magnificent sweep, after much local opposition to the plan. I do not think the landscape-historian can resent what he sees now. It is a fine road, and already a bit of history.

If you want to see what Charnwood looked like before it was tamed, Bradgate Park (now owned by the city and the county of Leicester jointly) preserves much of the natural appearance of a medieval hunting-park, with its fern and gorse, its ancient pollarded oaks, and outcrops of old stone here and there, and even deer in places. Though Bradgate was the scene of one of the first country houses in England, begun before 1500, and was lived in until the early

18th century, it did not last. The noble owners deserted the house for another in Staffordshire; Bradgate fell into ruin, and the old park was never subjected to the smoothing hands of the great landscapers; the rough bracken never yielded to green lawns and parkland in the Georgian idiom. Charnwood still retains a good many secret and beautiful places, but it is best avoided at week-ends and on fine Sundays.

In the crowded Midlands, swarming with people and cars, heavily built-up and pylon-studded, one is grateful for areas of space and quiet. The East Midlands are far less crowded than the West, and become more and more peaceful as one goes beyond the Soar towards Rutland and Lincolnshire. But even in the crowded parts there are two kinds of walking where one is free from traffic, noise, and people. The towpaths of the old canals in Leicestershire

make delightful walking, with room for picnics, and only the occasional fisherman in sight. Such canals can easily be found on the one-inch map. Particularly attractive stretches, miles of solitude and pastoral beauty, can be found in the south of the county from Kilby Bridge on the A.50 up through Newton Harcourt, Saddington, and on towards Foxton and Market Harborough. But these deserted canals can be found in all parts of the county and the best bits, once discovered, will prove a constant solace. They are the Leicestershire equivalent of the moors in the north and west of England.

The other peaceful walking is to be found along the old drove-roads. These take a little more finding: they are not obvious on the map, but any track uncoloured on the map and running more or less directly across country for miles is likely to be such a road—used by the drovers in the 18th century and earlier to drive their herds of cattle towards the great meat markets, eating as they drifted along. On the ground these roads or tracks usually have very wide grass verges at intervals, once used as overnight stops and now just right for picnics.

Leicestershire to many people means "hunting". It is the home of some of the most famous packs in England, perhaps the most famous—the Quorn, the Cottesmore, the Belvoir, the Atherstone, Fernie, and Pytchley.

People have always hunted, but not until about the 16th century was the uneatable fox regarded as worthy of pursuit. Before that it was the deer and the hare. There are references to fox-hunting in Henry VIII's time, but it was not really until the closing years of the 17th century that the sport began to be organised in Leicestershire. The first great name is Thomas Boothby, of Tooley Park, who is always said to have kept the first pack of fox-hounds in England. He hunted for fifty-five seasons, from 1698 to 1753, over country which later became identified with the Quorn. When he died, his place was taken by Hugo Meynell, who settled at Quorn and so gave the name to the most famous hunt of all. Meynell reigned from 1753 to 1800; the two

men between them ruled the field for just over 100 years.

The Cottesmore claims an equal longevity: it is not for the layman to adjudicate between these claims. Hounds were brought down to Rutland—to Cottesmore—in the closing years of the 17th century from Lowther in Westmorland. The Belvoir, once ruled from the castle, started about 1750. The territories of these three meet at Melton Mowbray, once—and I suppose still—the hunting metropolis of England. I have been told that before the Second World War a thousand fine hunters were brought to Melton at the beginning of the season, and the night air was sulphurous with aristocratic adultery.

The Quorn rules over north Leicestershire, the Cottesmore over the eastern side, the Belvoir on the north-east. The west of Leicestershire is mostly covered by the Atherstone, dating from about 1804, and the south by the Fernie (named after a dynasty of masters). A tiny bit of the extreme south of the county is hunted by the Pytchley, which is predominantly a Northamptonshire pack.

Whatever one may think of fox-hunting as a sport, it is one of the last survivals of the picturesque in England; it has produced some splendid literature; and it has dotted the English landscape with names that to their devotees cause a lifting of the heart—Billesdon Coplow, the Whissendine Brook, Ashby Pastures, Kirby Gate—but what can the layman know of these holy places? The meets are always well advertised in the local newspapers, but one should take care to avoid the well-known days when there are more cars than horses in the scene.

There is one more remarkable thing about this small county: it has created three magnificent foods in its time, gastronomic creations that have a national reputation. Some benighted parts of England have produced nothing of any note at all outside their boundaries and of precious little value inside them: but Leicester-

The Grand Union Canal
above Nr. Laughton
below Nr. Smeeton Westerby

shire has its Stilton cheese, its Leicestershire cheese, and its pork pies.

This part of England has long been famous for its bacon and pork—"Leicester beans and bacon, food of kings", they said in the 17th century (not my idea of royal food, though), and since the early years of the 19th century there have been the wonderful pork pies one dreams about in exile. It is true that neighbouring counties, like Nottinghamshire and Lincolnshire (even as far away as south Yorkshire) boast they make better pies, but I doubt it. My only uncertainty is whether the finest pies are made in Leicester (I am not allowed to say which shop, but everybody in Leicester knows it) or in Melton Mowbray (again one shop in particular, though not everyone would agree so readily here). Stamford, not so far away in Lincolnshire, does a very good pork pie too. At Melton, pork pies have been made on a commercial scale since the 1830s and have been the subject of a learned monograph by Mr Jack Brownlow of Melton. They say they do a good pie in Coalville also. If you have not known the pork pies of the east Midlands, but only the factory-made product, you have never really lived, gastronomically speaking.

As for Stilton cheese, named after a village on the old Great North Road (which is in Huntingdonshire), it is wholly a Leicestershire creation despite the name attached to it. Year after year this old query comes up, but the answer is quite certain. It was widely known in Leicestershire for decades before the landlord of the Bell at Stilton got to hear of it, obtained supplies, and made it famous to all who stopped at his inn on their coaching journeys. It became known henceforth as "Stilton", and so it is still called. The great Leicestershire historian, John Nichols, thought it the best cheese in the world.

Nichols tells us, writing about 1800, that it was first made at Little Dalby by Elizabeth Scarbrow, later Mrs Orton, who settled at

Dalby about 1720. But it was already known as Quenby cheese, from the lovely Jacobean house that still stands on the High Leicestershire grasslands; and even back at Quenby it was known as "Lady Beaumont's cheese", so we must look back further still. In *Midland England*, published twenty years ago, I discussed this knotty point and settled for the Mary Beaumont who lived at Kirby Bellars, not far from Quenby. The Jacobean house where she was born still stands beside the main road from Leicester to Melton.

In recent years the name Stilton began to be copied widely, like Cheddar or Champagne. The makers of the real thing fought a High Court action to protect their priceless name, and won it. Now it is properly applied only to the cheese made in a limited number of places—in Melton Mowbray, in certain villages in North Leicestershire, and in a few places just over the border in Nottinghamshire and Derbyshire. Like so many things, Stilton is supposed to be not what it was before the war, but a good Stilton is still something memorable.

The red Leicestershire cheese was made in the southern part of the county in the 18th and 19th centuries. There were apparently several local cheeses under this general label, and Mr Monk, the reporter to the Board of Agriculture in the 1790s, thought some of these better than Stilton. Down to 1939 the best "red Leicester" still came from the country south-west of Leicester, but the war and its rationing killed the farmhouse product, and the only genuine Leicester cheese is now made in a factory in Melton Mowbray.

Melton turns out to be, then, a place of gastronomic renown, for it makes Stilton and Leicester cheese, and also superb pork pies: three kinds of perfection in one small market town. There cannot be another town in Britain in this class.

Alas, though, Leicestershire does not live up

19

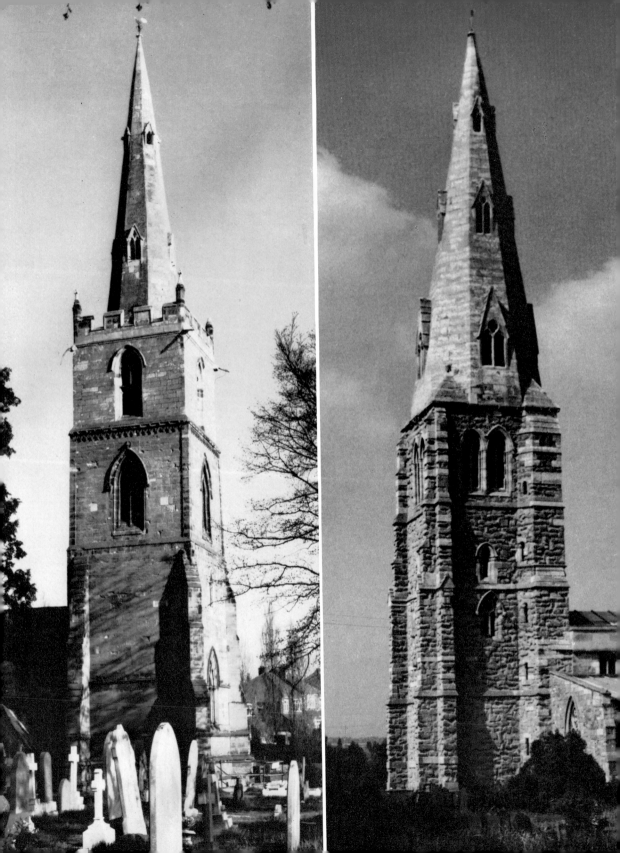

to this gastronomic level in its hotels and restaurants, and on the whole is not at all good. There is too much money and not enough taste in the Midlands. The quality of a meal is judged by the size of the bill or the height of the flames in some exhibitionist cooking at the table. One still eats best at home, and it is a minor torture to be compelled to eat out. English food at its best is the equal of anything anywhere in the world, and infinitely better than most countries. But it takes a good housewife to make it so, and such a wife is nowadays a pearl among women: indeed, rarer than a pearl.

BOSWORTH FIELD

Every schoolboy knows the name of Bosworth Field, one of the momentous battles which changed the course of English history. It was fought on an August morning in the placid countryside of west Leicestershire, about two miles to the south of the little town of Market Bosworth which gives the battle its name, though the actual site lies in the adjoining parish of Sutton Cheney.

Although the countryside has changed much since that date nearly 500 years ago, there is still a good deal to see for those gifted with some historical imagination, and it is well worth making a pilgrimage around this small piece of country.

Henry Tudor, Earl of Richmond, had landed at Milford Haven in the far west of Wales on 7 August 1485, and eventually reached Shrewsbury. From here, with his small army, he moved down Watling Street (now called the A.5) and by 20 August he had reached Atherstone. Meanwhile, King Richard III had left Nottingham for Leicester. Neither side knew where the enemy was to be found: indeed, discovering the whereabouts of the enemy in the absence of any modern means of communication must have been the major problem in medieval warfare; and the two armies, aided by the reports of scouts, moved very slowly towards each other.

On Wednesday, 17 August, Richard left Leicester, probably by what is now the Hinckley road, with an army of some 10,000 men. That evening his officers slept in the church at Elmesthorpe. The village itself had already disappeared and this was the only accommodation available. On the following day—Thursday, 18 August— Richard moved through Barwell and pitched camp on ground just south and south-west of Stapleton called The Bradshaws. This site used to be marked on the 1-inch map, but it has unfortunately been omitted from the new edition. For those using the new map, therefore, it is necessary to say that The Bradshaws lay between the Tweed river and the village of Stapleton, astride the present main road.

Here Richard and his armies remained from the Thursday until the evening of Sunday, 21 August, probably awaiting firm news of the whereabouts and movements of the enemy. Then they moved northwards through Stapleton towards the higher ground by Sutton Cheney, probably following the present track past the Manor Farm at Stapleton which was then a moated homestead. The remains of this moat can still be seen by the trackway. A field-path leads one on directly to Sutton Cheney, and there can be little doubt that Richard's army trudged along this path. At Sutton, Richard is said to have harangued his officers and men from a mound, and this, too, survives. Right between the road to Market Bosworth and that to Shenton, the highest ground hereabouts, is a large mound shown on the map as a Tumulus: here is the very place from which Richard spoke on the eve of battle.

From this point a long ridge, known as Ambion Hill, runs westwards towards Shenton, reaching a height of 400 ft. and commanding the surrounding countryside in all directions. Richard's three armies were drawn up on this hill on Sunday evening. The Duke of Norfolk's army occupied the western end of the hill, Richard's army the middle, just about where Ambion Hill Farm now stands, and the third army under the Duke of Northumberland was drawn up between this and Sutton Cheney.

In the meantime, Henry Tudor, still waiting at Atherstone for news of Richard's whereabouts, was informed by a neighbouring squire, John Hardwick of Lindley, where Richard lay. Hardwick and his retainers guided Henry for the last few miles towards the final battlefield. They came along the Roman road through Fenny Drayton for some miles until they reached the side-road running north towards Shenton. This road can be followed today: it is interesting to see how much the Roman roads survived as the best means of getting around even in the 15th century. On Sunday, 21 August, Henry's army halted for the night at White Moors, just south of Shenton village at a place which is still shown on the 1-inch map. Thus, on the eve of battle, the two armies lay for the night about a mile to a mile and a half apart, with Richard's armies on the hill some 120 ft. above Henry—a commanding start to have.

The battle was fought on the following morning, Monday, 22 August, and, thanks not a little to the treachery of the Stanleys, resulted in the defeat and death of Richard III. The fighting lasted only two hours: in that time the fate of England was decided. Henry's forces pursued the broken remnants of Richard's armies southwards towards Stoke Golding. It was here, just to the west of the village, on a hillock still known as Crown Hill, that one of the Stanleys placed on the head of Henry Tudor the crown which Richard had lost in the heat of the battle. The crown is traditionally said to have been found in a thorn-bush, and on the rough piece of ground to this day, too rough to build upon, gnarled thorn-trees still grow. This humdrum bit of waste ground is an historic piece of England—but how many people ever visit it?

So one can follow to this day, although the countryside has been much changed in some respects, a great part of the route followed by both armies in the three or four days before the final clash. The pilgrim should be warned, however, that the actual site where Richard's army lay on the eve of battle, at Ambion Hill Farm, is not a place where visitors are encouraged. This is unfortunate, for just south of the farm is King Richard's Well, where the king, in the heat of battle, drank at a spring. This spring is now covered by a small stone structure, and is marked as *Well* on the $2\frac{1}{2}$-inch map, and on the 1-inch map (Sheet 132) on the northern edge of Ambion Wood. Though access to the spring is barred through Ambion Hill Farm, I am told it can be approached from the opposite direction.

The number after each entry refers to the square on the map where the place is to be found

Ab Kettleby (5). High on south slope of the Leicestershire Wolds. Danish name "Ketil's *by*". Abbe was a late 12th-century owner—hence the village name. The church (St James) is of decayed ironstone like so many in this part of Leicestershire. Mostly 13th century but over-restored in 1851–3. North aisle is Victorian. Early English tower with 14th-century spire. Some late medieval benches (*c*. 1500). Original late medieval roof to chancel. Norman font (restored). Attractive setting with early 17th-century manor house nearby, of the usual ironstone.

Allexton (9). Tiny village beside the Eye Brook, here the frontier with Rutland. The church (St Peter) is basically Late Norman (1160–80). Splendid north arcade (*c*. 1160), rebuilt 1862, but accurately. Chancel

opposite APPLEBY MAGNA

below APPLEBY PARVA

arch a little later. The south arcade is Early English. Externally much restored—the aisles rebuilt 1863. Hall originally Elizabethan, later converted to a farmhouse and partly taken down in 1843, and then rebuilt in 1902. Grounds long famous for fine avenues of Balm of Gilead trees.

Anstey (5). Once "a neat village" but now swamped by Leicester. The church (St Mary) was rebuilt 1845–6 except the tower. Some early timber-framed houses remain. Packhorse bridge south of modern road bridge of 5 arches, probably late medieval in date. Ancestral village of the Martins since the 12th century, who still flourish not far away.

Appleby Magna (1), has a large and handsome early 14th-century church (St Michael) close to one of the best-preserved medieval moated sites in Leicestershire. The church was re-

stored in 1827: note the fine plaster rib-vault, box-pews, and gallery. Only the gatehouse survives of the 15th-century manor house, to which is attached a picturesque timber-framed house of 16th-century date. Some 16th–17th-century houses in village.

Appleby Parva (1). Striking grammar school in small village, built 1693–7 at the cost of Sir John Moore, who had made a fortune in the East India trade. He was Lord Mayor of London, 1681; M.P. for the City, 1685. The school was designed by Sir William Wilson; Wren had made an earlier design. Built for boys in villages round about, but in 1706 "it was made free for all England" and is still used as a school. Statue of Sir John Moore by Wilson (1701) wearing wig and hat.

Arnesby (8) (St Peter) is basically a Norman church, the two fine

arcades being early 12th century, but chancel, south aisle and west tower are all early 14th century. Over-restored 1868. Birthplace of Rev. Robert Hall, Baptist divine (1764–1831), whose father was minister here. Chapel founded 1667, rebuilt 1702 and now the garage to the Manse (also 1702). Present chapel 1799. Moated homestead site south-east of church. Remains of moat still visible, and the house still stood in the 1860s—"an ancient timbered dwelling with mud walls and a thatched roof".

Arnesby formerly had a market and an eight-day fair, granted to Hugh le Despencer in 1292, which fell out of use long ago. The A.50 road was then the chief medieval route between Leicester and Northampton.

Asfordby (5) could be described fifty years ago as "a pretty village in the Wreake valley". No one could call it that today, though it retains a number of handsome houses. The church (All Saints) is mostly 14th century, with 15th-century tower and clerestory. Note the 15th-century nave roof, supported by wooden angels with instruments. Also a Saxon stone in the west wall of the north transept, part of a 10th-century carved cross-shaft.

Good Georgian rectory house (1808), and Jacobean brick-built hall in village. Asfordby Hall, "a large and handsome mansion", was built in the Italian style in 1840 at a cost of about £4,000: happy days.

Five blast-furnaces using the local iron ore helped to create the unlovely part known as Asfordby Hill in the last quarter of the 19th century.

Ashby-de-la-Zouch (1) was described in White's *Directory* for 1846 as "a handsome and highly salubrious *market town* and *watering place*, celebrated for its *saline baths* and the extensive remains of its once formidable and famous baronial Castle. . . ." First of all, though, its charming name: Ashby is common enough in Leicestershire where the ash-tree has always flourished, and Zouch comes from its manorial lords, la Zouch being an ancient Breton family who acquired Ashby

about the year 1160. There is a splendidly bad poem by Lady Flora Hastings entitled "Ashby de la Zouch", published in Blackwood's Magazine in 1841 and reprinted in a *Guide to Ashby-de-la-Zouch* (1863).

Although the Leicestershire coalfield is not far away, Ashby remains a pleasant little town and there is much to see. Market Street takes its name from the weekly market granted as long ago as 1219, the market now held on Saturdays. There used also to be no fewer than four annual fairs. Visually the most rewarding part of the town, as Nikolaus Pevsner says, is the Spa quarter beyond the west end of Market Street. This originated in the discovery of a copious saline spring when working coal at Moira Colliery, 3 miles west of the town in 1805. Here the Moira Baths were erected, with a commodious hotel nearby; but after a few years these proved insufficient and the water was conveyed to Ashby. The *Ivanhoe Baths* were erected in 1822, with a Doric façade 200 ft. long. These, despite local feeling, have recently been destroyed. The *Royal Hotel* was built in 1826 to accommodate visitors to the growing spa; this still survives (1969) with "a handsome, small central hall with Doric columns" (Pevsner). The pleasing little railway station of 1849 is now deserted and mouldering away. The Free Grammar School, founded in the reign of Edward VI, formerly occupied a school-house built in 1807, now also destroyed.

The architectural centre of Ashby is, however, the parish church of St Helen and the splendid castle, grouped together on the south side of the town. The church is mainly late 15th century in date, probably built at the same time as the castle, for Lord Hastings was one of the richest men of his time (c. 1430–83) and one of the foremost builders. Additions were made to the church in 1878 (e.g. the outer arcades). In the Hastings Chapel there is a fine alabaster monument to the 2nd Earl of Huntingdon (d. 1561), and another monument to the 9th Earl (d. 1746), designed by William Kent. Other monuments include those of Selina (d. 1791) the Countess of Huntingdon who founded the well-

known Connexion and was a notable figure in 18th-century nonconformity; and the 2nd Marquess of Hastings (d. 1844). In the north aisle is the alabaster effigy of a pilgrim (15th century). The Roman Catholic church is by F. Walters, 1908–15.

The castle is of various dates. A Norman manor house which originally stood here was reconstructed and added to c. 1350 to form a long range of domestic buildings running east and west for 90 yards. The kitchen (at the west end) is one of the best of its kind. The great hall, on the usual plan of a nave and two aisles, was originally part of the 12th-century house, but was much altered c. 1350 and again in the early 17th century. Beyond the hall are the remains of the solar and the chapel, both largely of mid-14th-century date. In 1476 Lord Hastings built the great tower-house, a self-contained fortress necessary at a time when the revival of private warfare threatened to jeopardise the lives and property of great and hated overlords. Hastings himself was summarily beheaded in 1483 (*see also Kirby Muxloe*). In the Civil Wars the fortress held out for fifteen months for the King (1644–6) and in 1648 it was ordered by Parliament to be slighted; but the ruins are still very impressive. Among the royal visitors to Ashby Castle were Mary Queen of Scots, James I, and Charles I.

Ashby Folville (5) lies beside a typical Leicestershire stream, embosomed in fine trees. The church (St Mary) is mostly 1300–30, with the usual perpendicular tower and clerestory. Font Norman. Incised slab in chancel to 15th-century squire, Ralph Woodford, and monuments to George Smith (1607), Francis Smith (1629). Their manor house, "a large stone mansion in the Gothic style", sank in the social scale to a farmhouse by the early 19th century, but was largely rebuilt in the 1890s and upgraded again—all this a fairly common sequence in Leicestershire.

Ashby Pastures (by the road to Melton) is one of "the oldest and best Quorn covers". Like a number of famous fox-covers in Leicestershire, this started as an allotment of a cow-pasture to the poor of the parish, decayed out of recognition,

16th century, built by the Vernons, who owned the manor until 1565. Said to have been the abode of Charles I during the siege of Leicester in May 1645. It now belongs to the City of Leicester; grounds open to the public.

The church (St Andrew) has a splendid chancel, c. 1300, one of the largest village chancels in England. Fine brass to William Heathcott, rector (d. 1595). Jacobean poor-box (1613). Rest of church 13th-15th century. The Saxon window in the tower (which is 13th century) is an archaeological mystery.

Note the medieval pack-horse bridge over the river, probably 15th century in date.

Baggrave (5) now only a mid-Georgian hall in an attractive small park. It was once a village with its own church, but was deserted c. 1500 and disappeared. The site of the village lies due south of the hall. A small moated area marks the site of the medieval manor house.

Bagworth (4) is an unlovely coal-mining village with good views, however, of the western edge of Charnwood Forest. Coal was discovered here in 1826 and the formerly picturesque countryside was duly devastated. The old church (Holy Rood) was mainly Norman and Early English, and was rebuilt in 1873 except its rough little tower which could well be a late 11th-century structure. Under threat of demolition at present (1967).

Bardon Hill (4) is the highest point of Charnwood Forest (912 ft.), now extensively wooded. According to Murray's *Handbook* one could see from here the Shropshire and Derbyshire hills and on occasion even the Sugarloaf in Monmouthshire and the Malvern Hills in Worcestershire. White's *Directory* (1846) says the whole range of vision embraced an area of 5,000 sq. miles.

Barkby (5) has been the home of the Pochins since 1633 when they bought the manor. The hall is "a large plain mansion in a well-wooded park", built in 1810 and added to in the mid-19th century. The church (St Mary) is ironstone, mainly 13th

then planted for hunting, a rent being paid by the hunt to the apathetic owners of common rights.

Ashby Magna (8) church (St Mary) has been heavily restored (1861 onwards) and part rebuilt (1907). Some 13th-century work remains in the north arcade and aisle.

Ashby Parva (7) church (St Peter) mostly perpendicular. Tower rebuilt 1889, chancel 1868, but a Norman font survives. Some interesting houses in village, especially almshouses of 1832.

Aston Flamville (7) church (St Peter) was almost rebuilt in 1873–4; a Norman window in the north wall shows what was lost. Incised slab to Sir William Turville (1552) and wife. The manor has belonged to a succession of great families—Flamville, Hastings, Mowbray, Turville, and Ashby. Manor house 18th century, with dovecote of 1715. Nichols, the historian of Leicestershire, says, "Aston has long been famed for the luxuriance of its pastures and consequent excellence of its dairies; the cheese from this village bearing always a superior price in Leicester market".

Aylestone (8) on the east side of the Soar (and the Grand Union Canal) was once a pleasant village but is now engulfed in Greater Leicester. The *Hall* looks Victorian but its core is century, with some unique window tracery (early Decorated). Some Pochin monuments. The Pochins still flourish at the hall. In their Victorian heyday they owned some 7,800 acres and a rent-roll of rather more than £14,000 a year.

Barkestone (3) lies in the Vale of Belvoir, with fine views of the wooded escarpment to south and south-east. The deserted Grantham Canal (opened 1793, closed 1929) lies just outside the village. The church (St Peter and St Paul) is mostly perpendicular (*c.* 1500) but was drastically restored in 1840. Good screen and four richly carved stall-ends of *c.* 1500.

Barlestone (4), 3 miles north-east of Market Bosworth, has a church (St Giles) rebuilt, except the chancel, in 1855 by Benjamin Ferrey.

Barrow-upon-Soar (5) is mostly a large and dreary red-brick village, but several more interesting buildings are tucked away in side-streets. Note Dr Humphrey Babington's hospital (completed 1694) for six poor men, "widowers or antient bachelors". Dr Humphrey Perkins founded here a free school, 1717. Almshouses of 1825 in Tudor style.

William Beveridge, bishop of St Asaph, was born here 1636: "his writings highly esteemed by the clergy".

The church (Holy Trinity) is mostly a vigorous rebuilding or restoration of 1862-70. Altar rails 17th century. Monument to Martha Utber, 1745. Nave roof with good figures of angels.

A hard blue limestone is found here, esteemed since medieval times. The lime "fixes immediately in water" and much was exported to Holland, as well as used locally.

Barsby (5), a small hill-top village along a street which once formed part of a direct route between Gaddesby and Twyford. Its church "went to decay several centuries ago". Several interesting early brick houses, dated 1691-1707.

Barton-in-the-Beans (4) has apparently never had a church. Baptist chapel founded 1745, rebuilt in 1841. Barton is said to have been the earli-

est chapel of the General Baptists in this part of the Midlands. As for the beans (a great crop in medieval Leicestershire and later) a writer in 1720 said they "are so luxuriant that they appear like a forest towards harvest-time".

Barwell (7), a large red-brick manufacturing village. The church (St Mary) is a fine Decorated building (all 1300–40). Note roof with large corbel-heads, and good window tracery. Mural monument to Richard Breton, 1659.

Beacon Hill (4), rising to 818 ft., is the second highest hill in Charnwood. The summit can be reached from Woodhouse Eaves. It seems to have been a habitation site in the Early and Late Bronze Age. Commands wide views of the surrounding forest, and of the Soar and Trent valleys as far as Nottingham.

Beaumanor Park (4) on the north-eastern edge of Charnwood Forest is now a large house of 1840-7 in the Jacobean style, in a large park which was probably once a medieval hunting-park. The beauty of the site is reflected in its name ("beautiful place"). It belonged to Hugh, Earl of Chester, in 1086; later it belonged to the Beaumonts. In 1594 it was sold to William Herrick, a Leicester man who had made a fortune in London as a goldsmith-banker, and remained the seat of the Herricks down to the Second World War. The park formerly occupied nearly the whole manor. In Victorian days the Perry-Herricks were among the lordliest landowners in Leicestershire, owning nearly 14,000 acres in four counties and a rent-roll of over £22,000 a year. The mansion was bought by the War Office in 1947.

Beeby (5) is a small village, curiously remote though so near suburban Leicester. Large green with some good houses (e.g. The Grange, and the Manor House). It was once much larger than now. There was a church here as long ago as the 10th century, belonging to Crowland Abbey. The present church (All Saints) is remarkable for its handsome tower with an unfinished truncated steeple, the subject of various legends. One is

that the builders were two brothers who quarrelled on the job. One threw the other off the scaffold and then in remorse threw himself down. Another is that the builder despaired of rivalling the beautiful spire of Queniborough not far away and threw himself from the battlements. Or it may be simply that the money ran out and the work was left unfinished. Spacious 14th-century interior with usual Perpendicular clerestory. Curious 13th-century font. Note also the medieval faces on the stone corbels, and 14th-century rood-screen: altogether a pleasing country interior. Chancel rebuilt meanly in 1819. "Near the church is a well of beautiful water over which [in 1855] was built a sort of pyramid" with an inscription. This was undoubtedly the aboriginal water supply of the ancient village, the reason why it is here.

Belgrave (5), once a country village, then a good residential suburb for wealthy Leicester tradespeople, and now engulfed by the northward red-brick sprawl of the city, retains a fragment of its ancient peace and beauty in Church Road. Belgrave Hall (built 1709-13) is, as Jack Simmons says in his excellent *Guide to the City of Leicester*, the best house of its period within the city boundaries. It now belongs to the city and is used most attractively as a museum. On the other side of the road is Belgrave House built in 1776, and now used for museum purposes. The parish church (St Peter) has been over-restored but retains traces of its Norman origin in the lower part of the tower (the top stage is early 16th-century) and a fine south doorway. Note also the 14th-century chancel windows, and the sedilia of the same date. On the way to Belgrave (along the dreary Belgrave Road) is the Victorian church of St Mark (1870–2) by Ewan Christian, largely built of Swithland slate. Impressive, with a spire that is a landmark in these flat northern wastes of Leicester, but no longer used.

Belton (4) used to have a weekly market and a notable horse fair, granted to Gracedieu Priory as early as 1243. Part of the village is still called the Market Place. The horse fair used to be the largest in the county. The church (St John the Baptist) is mostly a Decorated building, with a Perpendicular clerestory and roof. The alabaster monument is that of Roesia de Verdun, who founded Gracedieu Priory for nuns, not far away, about 1239, and the monument is of about that date. Pevsner, however, points out that since alabaster was not in use as early as this, the effigy and its surround may be a later copy. The tomb was formerly at Gracedieu (*q.v.*) and was brought to Belton at the Dissolution in 1539.

Belvoir (3) (pronounced *Beever*) has been called "perhaps the lordliest place in England, Windsor Castle alone excepted". The castle, set on the end of a bold escarpment some 200 ft. above the Vale which takes its name, was first built by Robert de Todeni, a standard-bearer of William the Conqueror, in the closing decades of the 11th century. The name is first recorded in 1130 as *Belveder* and in 1145 as *Bello Videre*, "beautiful view", from the enormous tract of country it commands. Seen from the Vale below, the castle (which was largely rebuilt in 1800–30) is spectacular. A closer view can be had

from the hillside road which runs from Belvoir towards Woolsthorpe, when "its towers, turrets, and crenellations [make it] much the *beau idéal* of the romantic castle" (Pevsner). There are purists, however, who think it romantically ugly with its too-good-to-be-true Mixed Medieval outline.

The Manners family from Northumberland (now dukes of Rutland) inherited Belvoir by marriage when it was ruinous. The first earl of Rutland (created 1525) began rebuilding the castle in 1528, turning it from a fortress into a dwelling-house. This suffered great damage in the Civil

BELVOIR castle

War, and the eighth earl built a mansion on the site in c. 1654–68. In 1800 the fifth duke (the dukedom had been created in 1703) and his duchess decided to remodel this plain block-like house into the likeness of a medieval castle. James Wyatt was employed as architect until his death in 1813. The work was carried to completion by the Vicar of Bottesford (Sir John Thoroton) who was also chaplain to the duke. A great fire in 1816 destroyed most of the completed building, but Thoroton set to work again with the help of Wyatt's two sons, and the castle was finally completed about 1830. It is open to the public on certain days of the week and is, of course, one of the show-places of the Midlands. The mausoleum, built 1826–8 in the Norman style, has an impressive interior. Here are the more recent tombs of the family, the earlier ones forming a splendid sequence in the chancel of Bottesford church (q.v.).

The dovecote in the grounds stands on the site of Belvoir Priory, founded by Robert de Todeni about 1076–88 and suppressed in 1539. It was a small Benedictine cell of the great abbey at St Albans, for four monks only.

The country around Belvoir, with its splendid woods, steep and broken hillsides, deep valleys and artificial lakes round Knipton, is quite unlike any other scenery in Leicestershire and is justly popular among motorists at week-ends.

Bescaby (6) lies 1½ miles north-east of Waltham-on-the-Wolds, in quiet unfrequented country 500 ft. above sea-level. The river Eye (which becomes the Wreak below Melton) rises here in Hamwell Spring and soon forms a moated manor-house site with a fine fishpond of the same date (probably 13th-century). The moated site, one of the best in the county, is now uninhabited and densely overgrown. There were formerly a chapel and a village here, but both disappeared before 1500. The site of the village is marked by low earthen banks in a field to the south of the track leading

below and opposite Monuments in BOTTESFORD church

from the public road to Bescaby Farm.

Billesdon (5), a large and attractive village on the Leicester–Uppingham main road, derives its name from "Bill's hill". There can be little doubt that the hill referred to is the beautiful wooded eminence (some 700 ft. above sea-level) now called Billesdon Coplow, one of the few prominent landmarks in Leicestershire and a holy place in the annals of fox-hunting. Billesdon Coplow House was built shortly before 1790 and enlarged in the early 1840s. In the 1840s, too, the house was occupied by Thomas Tomblin, popularly called Capt. Tomblin, reputed to be "the cleverest 'rough rider' in the world".

The church (St John the Baptist) is basically a 13th-century building, but much rebuilt in the 1860s (tower and south aisle). The charming little village school (ironstone, 1650) stands in the older part of the village. Billesdon was granted a weekly market on Fridays in 1618, together with two annual fairs, but all have long been discontinued.

Birstall (5), an old village with a few vernacular cottages near the church, was in the 1840s a pleasant commuter village for Leicester businessmen. It has now been utterly swamped by the sprawl of the modern city. The church (St James) has a tower of 13th-century date. The nave was rebuilt 1828 and then "restored" by Scott in 1860. There are, however, some remains of the Anglo-Saxon church (e.g. a window in the north wall of the chancel and a carved stone of early 11th-century date nearby, with a "beast pattern").

Bitteswell (7) was described in the 1840s as "a large village with several handsome houses". Many of these remain, grouped around a large green. The Hall, "an elegant mansion", was built in 1838–9. The church (St Mary) has a tower of c. 1300, but the rest was vigorously restored in the early 1880s and is exceedingly dull today.

Blaby (8), a large village mostly of 19th–20th-century red-brick building but retaining a few more vernacular houses. Best of these is *The Baker's Arms*, an attractive thatched and timber-framed building claiming to date from 1485, which may well be true. The Grand Union Canal runs just north of the village, and on the north side of this again an Anglo-Saxon cemetery of 6th-century date was unearthed in 1866–71.

The church (All Saints) is mainly of late 13th–early–14th-century date, with a 16th-century clerestory. The rather dull interior is relieved by a handsome west gallery of about 1740. The nave was re-roofed in 1846, the chancel less satisfactorily in 1858, all during the incumbency of the Rev. Henry James Hoskins. The south aisle roof is dated 1630.

Blaby Hall, near the church, was built "in the Elizabethan style" in 1838, on the site of an earlier hall demolished in the preceding year.

Blackfordby (1) used to have a small Early English church, completely swept away by a new church (St Margaret) in 1857–58. The village stands high, commanding views from Cannock Chase to Charnwood Forest, including (so it is said) the spires of Lichfield Cathedral and no fewer than 25 village churches.

Blaston (9) (pronounced Blayston) is a tiny village in the attractive upland country towards the Rutland border. There are two churches, neither now of much interest. Blaston St Giles was rebuilt by G. E. Street in 1878, but possesses a pre-Reformation chalice of c. 1500, much repaired in 1842. Blaston St Michael was rebuilt in 1867–8 and is now derelict. Pleasant village street with some decent ironstone houses, including a good group of cottages (1647, well rebuilt in 1907).

Blaston Hall (still shown on the map) was built in the 1790s but was demolished c. 1930.

Priory Farm, a mile east of Blaston, is an early 19th-century farmhouse, taking its name from the small Augustinian priory of Bradley, founded shortly before 1190 and dissolved in 1536. The site of the priory can be seen near the farmhouse, and is marked by slight mounds and depressions. It never had more than three or four canons, and only two when it came to an end.

Bottesford (3) is a large village in the extreme north-east corner of Leicestershire with some attractive Georgian houses here and there. But the glory of the place is the parish church (St Mary), and here above all the splendid monuments of eight earls of Rutland, one of the finest sights of its kind in England outside London. The church itself looks externally mostly Decorated and Perpendicular with a 13th-century chancel and north transept of early 14th-century. The south aisle and south porch are 1330–50, the south transept somewhat later again. Pulpit and reading desk, 1631. The spire (210 ft.) is the highest in Leicestershire.

In the chancel are the monuments of the eight earls, lords of Belvoir, on the escarpment to the south. A full description of these will be found in the excellent church guide. Here one can only give the barest details:

Thomas, 1st earl (d. 1543) and wife, tomb by Richard Parker of Burton-on-Trent

Henry, 2nd earl (d. 1563) and wife

Edward, 3rd earl (d. 1587) and wife, by Gerard Johnson of Southwark

John, 4th earl (d. 1588) and wife, by Nicholas Johnson

Roger, 5th earl (d. 1612) and wife, by Nicholas Johnson

Francis, 6th earl (d. 1632) and two wives

George, 7th earl (d. 1641) by Grinling Gibbons (long after the earl's death)

John, 8th earl (d. 1679) and wife, by Grinling Gibbons.

Of these tombs, Nikolaus Pevsner selects that of the 6th earl as "the grandest of the Bottesford tombs", but the author of the church guide calls it "a mass of pretentious vulgarity, both in its design and its inscription". It can only be said that this kind of sculpture easily arouses such opposing views. Much Elizabethan and Jacobean work both in architecture and sculpture strikes me as exceedingly vulgar: it was, after all, an age of the New Rich; though one could not apply this description to the noble lords of Belvoir. The inscription on the tomb alleges that two sons of the earl died as a result of sorcery, which led to the famous trial in 1619 of the so-called Witches of Belvoir, a classic in the history of

32

witchcraft. When the mausoleum was built at Belvoir in 1828, the bodies of the 9th earl (1st Duke of Rutland) and later dukes were transferred from Bottesford to there. There are earlier memorials, however, which should not be overlooked in studying the magnificent Rutland tombs. The brass of Henry Codyngton, rector of Bottesford (1404) is justly famous; and the diminutive effigy of Robert de Roos (1285), an earlier lord of Belvoir, should also be noticed.

Bradgate Park (4), one of several medieval hunting-parks round the edge of Charnwood Forest, is 820 acres in extent and is enclosed by a stone wall 4½ miles around. It now belongs to the city of Leicester and the county of Leicestershire and is open to the public. It owes its beauty to the fact that, though it belonged for generations to the Greys, who built a great house here, it was never "landscaped" but was left in its natural state of rugged rocks, bracken and ancient oak-trees. Herds of deer still roam the lower ground.

Early in the 12th century the earls of Leicester and Chester divided between them the greater part of Charnwood Forest. Bradgate was certainly enclosed for hunting before 1247. The park is highly picturesque, rising to 700 ft. at Old John—a tower built by the fifth earl of Stamford as a memorial to an old retainer of the family in 1786. Cropston reservoir, on the east side of the park, adds greatly to the natural beauty of the scenery here. The former village of Bradgate, deserted about 1500, lay on the south-east side of the reservoir. The ruins of Bradgate House, built by Thomas Grey, Marquis of Dorset, between about 1490 and 1505, are spectacular. The house, built largely of brick, was among the very first of the true "country houses" to be built in England. Lady Jane Grey was born here in October 1537. It was here that Roger Ascham found her reading Greek when he visited Bradgate in 1550. When she was executed in 1554 it is said that the foresters topped all the oaks in the park, so accounting for the pollarded oaks which are such a feature of the park today. The house was enlarged in the 17th century and William III was

entertained here in 1696. The Greys abandoned Bradgate in the 1730s for their house at Enville in Staffordshire and it fell into ruin. In the chapel, which is completely preserved (modern roof) is the tomb of Henry Grey, first earl of Stamford (d. 1673) and his wife.

Branston (3), in the tumbled landscape of the upper Devon valley, is a pleasant village in the Belvoir country. The church (St Cuthbert) is the usual Leicestershire 13th century with 15th-century additions, the font late Norman with intersecting arcade. Modern directories say the church is dedicated to St Guthlac. It was much restored at various dates in the 19th century.

Braunstone (5) could once be described as "a pleasant village" but is now utterly swamped by the westward sprawl of Leicester. As recently as 1924 the *Little Guide* could call it "a curiously remote and isolated little village, with stately Hall of brick, in a pretty park with water". The vast housing estates created here led to the unfortunate extensions of the old parish church (St Peter) so that the main axis now runs north-south. The 15th-century chancel screen has survived these fearful changes. As for the hall, built for the Winstanleys in 1775 by a local architect, it is now used as a school, and the park is a public open space. There are traces of the old village in a few timber-framed farmhouses and cottages. Most of Braunstone was bought by the Leicester Corporation in 1925 for development as a housing estate.

Breedon-on-the-Hill (4) is one of the most fascinating places in Leicestershire. Here we have an ancient monastic site within the ramparts of an Iron Age hill-fortress. The hill is a massive block of carboniferous limestone, rising nearly 200 ft. above the surrounding country and commanding fine views of the Trent valley and of Charnwood Forest. Breedon derives its name from this limestone rock, the British word for "hill" being *Bre-*, to which the Old English (not knowing the older word) added their own *dun*, with the same meaning.

The hill was crowned by the strongest earthwork in Leicestershire, constructed between the 1st century B.C. and the 1st century A.D. The ramparts, known locally as The Bulwarks, have been destroyed on the east and south sides by long-continued quarrying. The fact that a monastery was founded on the hill-top, far above the village and most inconvenient for it, suggests that the site may have had a religious significance in pre-Christian times. It was taken over for the first Christian church in the last quarter of the 7th century, probably as part of the great missionary activity from Peterborough to whom Breedon had been given by the King of Mercia in the year 680. The monks of Peterborough are known to have erected the church at Brixworth in Northamptonshire about 670, a church which still stands and which has been described as "perhaps the most imposing architectural memorial of the 7th century yet surviving north of the Alps". The early monastery at Breedon was probably destroyed by the Danes in the late 9th century, but the monks must have hidden the remarkable carved friezes that we see today and so preserved them for posterity. These have been dated as late 8th century. About 60 ft. of frieze survives in the present church, consisting of carved ornament representing "ivy-vine scrolls, human, beast, and bird figures in considerable variety, and a number of panels of geometrical ornament" (Sir Alfred Clapham). This Mercian sculpture is unlike anything else in Europe. The most beautiful figure is that of an angel, about 3 ft. high.

The story of the existing church (St Mary and St Hardulph) is a somewhat complicated one as, in addition to the parish church, an Augustinian priory was founded on the same site *c.* 1120 as a cell of Nostell priory in Yorkshire. It was always a very small house, beginning with a prior and five canons but dwindling to only two canons shortly before its dissolution *c.* 1540. It is difficult to work out the relationship of the priory church to the parish church since everything west of the present tower has disappeared, as is evidenced by the arch in the west wall of the tower. A few traces of the 12th-century

C

church can be seen in the lower part of the tower (e.g. typical buttresses, and some deeply-splayed windows in north and south walls of the tower). Pevsner thinks that the next step was to add a parochial nave to the Norman tower (to the west), and that in the 13th century a long-aisled chancel was built to the east of the tower. When the original nave was destroyed, this chancel became the nave of the parish church. This change probably took place at the dissolution of the priory, as the whole church would have been too large for the village below. In the 14th century the original aisle windows were replaced, except the fine 13th-century lancets in the east walls. A Perpendicular clerestory was added in the usual way.

The furnishings of the church are also of considerable interest—18th-century box-pews, pulpit and reading-desk, and west gallery; the Shirley pew dated 1627; and three alabaster tombs in the Shirley Chapel—John Shirley of Staunton Harold (d. 1570), Francis Shirley and his wife (both d. 1571), and George Shirley (d. 1588) and his wife. In the village itself is a circular stone lock-up for 17th-century wrongdoers.

Brentingby (6) is now little more than a disused church and a small manor house in the gentle valley of the Eye. The church (dedication unknown) has a saddle-back west tower (early 14th-century): the rest was rebuilt about the same time that the nearby Hall was built (in the 1650s). Brentingby was never a large place, but there must be the signs of a "lost village" somewhere close by. The directory of 1846 says "here is a chalybeate spring, said to resemble that at Scarborough".

Bringhurst (9) used to be a tiny hill-top village but has grown a little recently. It is obviously an ancient site, with the church (St Nicholas) standing at the highest and most central point. A church existed here well before the Norman Conquest. It was the mother-church of Great Easton, now much larger and grander. Despite its external appearance it is still basically a 12th-century church, with a good Late Norman north arcade. The south aisle was added c. 1250. Some repair work in 17th-century (cf. windows and porch).

Some good 17th-century houses near the church. Fine views up and down the broad Welland valley, and across to Rockingham Castle.

Brooksby (5), in the Wreak valley, was until recently little more than a church, a hall, and a deserted village site; but the hall is now an Agricultural Institute and the village has regrown. The earlier village seems to have been depopulated by the latter half of the 14th century, probably as a consequence of the Black Death.

Brooksby Hall, the home of the Villers or Villiers family for many centuries, has traces of its Tudor origin, some early Georgian work and a larger extension made in 1891. The Villiers were lords of Brooksby from the early 13th century (perhaps before that) down to 1711, the last of the line to live here being Sir William Villiers, and his wife, whose fine monument is to be seen in the church. George Villiers, later Duke of Buckingham and the unscrupulous favourite of James I and Charles I, was born here in 1592. When the

Detail from the pre-Conquest frieze at BREEDON-ON-THE-HILL

BRINGHURST churchyard

Brooksby estate was sold after the death of the last Villiers, it went to Sir Nathan Wright, Lord Keeper, who is said to have amassed a large fortune by the corrupt disposal of patronage. In the mid-19th century Lord Cardigan, the "hero" of the Charge of the Light Brigade, another detestable character, retired here from active service. After the First World War, Brooksby became the home of Admiral Lord Beatty (1871–1936) of Jutland fame. He was Commander-in-Chief of the Grand Fleet 1916–19 and First Sea Lord 1919–27. Few great houses can have had such a fascinating social history as Brooksby.

The church (St Michael) is a pretty little building in the grounds of the Hall. There are no aisles, merely a nave and chancel dating from the early 14th century to the early 16th century. Besides the Villiers' monument already referred to, there is an incised slab to William Villers, esquire, dated 1481, between his two wives. It is strange that there are so few memorials in the church of such an ancient family.

Broughton Astley (7) has a fine church (St Mary), mostly early 14th-century in date, but the chancel was practically rebuilt in 1882. The nave and north aisle are of almost equal height and width. Note especially the Decorated tracery of the east window of the aisle. Much remodelling of the church in the Perpendicular period. In the porch, a Norman stoup.

Bruntingthorpe (8) lies in pleasant upland country south of Leicester, well worth exploration on a summer evening. The parish church (St Mary) was rebuilt in 1873, but retains an altar piece representing Christ being taken down from the Cross, painted by the Rev. Thomas Freeman, the then rector (d. 1834) who was a member of the Royal Academy. In the 19th century the village had the usual chalybeate spring and framework-knitters.

Buckminster (6) stands high on the little plateau between the infant river Witham and the Eye, just off the prehistoric trackway known as the Drift or Sewstern Lane. The name means "Bucca's *minster*", probably an early *monasterium* or mother-church for a wide area around. The Georgian parishioners of Buckminster believed that their church spire was the first sight of England by homeward-bound mariners on the North Sea.

The present church (St John

Baptist) is of massive grey limestone, 13th-century tower with later broach spire. Mostly a 14th-century interior (Decorated Gothic), but the chancel was remodelled in Perpendicular times. Late medieval timber roof on large corbel-heads. Remarkable octagonal stone staircase in the nave. In the north aisle is a painting of the Adoration of the Magi by Garofalo (1481–1559). Ugly Dysart mausoleum in churchyard.

The earls of Dysart lived at Buckminster Hall—built 1798, now demolished except for large stables by the road. The village is large and handsome, an "estate village" with the air of Victorian opulence, as well

it might have when the Dysarts drew some £45,000 a year from their 27,000 acres of land.

Burbage (7) stands on a hill, the church spire visible from afar. The church (St Catherine) was rebuilt in 1842 "in the modern Gothic style". Perfect half-timbered Elizabethan yeoman's house in a *cul-de-sac* south of the church. In Church Street several good Georgian houses. Nichols says "The village of Burbach was formerly the residence of several respectable families. . . . Among these were the names of Wightman, St Nicholas, Allington, Swift, Barnewell, Armeston, Boddington, Farmer,

and Watts. Not less than six coaches were once kept here; but the rage of figuring in the Metropolis, and the great increase of the stocking manufactory at Hinckley, seem to have brought on the declension of Burbach". The village was particularly prosperous in the 17th century. The hearth tax return of 1666 shows no fewer than a dozen large houses, occupied by substantial yeomen and gentry. In the church is a fine inscribed slab to Richard Wightman (1578) and two wives. In the chancel is a monument to the 9th Earl of Kent, 50 years rector of the parish (1643). Burbage is now mostly a "hosiery village", with much unlovely red-brick, but is better worth visiting than most places round about. Burbage House was rebuilt in 1842 as "a handsome Gothic mansion". George Canning, the stateman (1770–1827), resided in Burbage for a time and "employed himself in the cultivation of a few acres of land in the village when his parliamentary duties permitted".

Burrough-on-the-Hill (6) stands nearly 600 ft. above sea-level on the marlstone escarpment of east Leicestershire. The great earthwork of Burrough Hill is the grandest Iron Age hill-fort in the county and may well have been the capital of the Coritani before Leicester took over this function as *Ratae Coritanorum* in early Roman times.

The church (St Mary) is almost all of the 13th century, with a Decorated south aisle and doorway. Some decent ironstone farmhouses in the village of 17th- and 18th-century date. Cheseldyne Farm, north of the church, was the birthplace of William Cheselden (1688–1752), the eminent surgeon and anatomist. He was surgeon to Queen Anne and invented the lateral operation for the stone.

Burton Lazars (6), a hill-top village south of Melton, takes its second name from the fact that here was founded the largest and richest leper hospital in England. It was founded before 1146 and suppressed just four hundred years later. Nothing remains of the buildings, but extensive

Squires tomb, BURTON LAZARS

BURROUGH-ON-THE-HILL, the iron-age ramparts

earthworks may be seen about 350 yards west of the church, chiefly the moats which surrounded the hospital and a fine series of fishponds for the treatment of the disease.

The parish church (St James) stands beside the main road. Its western bellcote with small saddleback tower and spire is typical of several churches in the Melton district. Internally, the south arcade has round arches with water-leaf capitals to the piers (late 12th-century); the north arcade is somewhat later. The 15th-century roof has minstrels holding musical instruments. In the churchyard is the ostentatious tomb of a weaver named William Squires (1780)—nearly all his money went on this memorial. Also, tombs of two counts Zborowski, father and son, killed in motor-racing 1909, 1924. Some good Swithland slate headstones also.

Burton-on-the-Wolds (5) has a late Georgian hall, formerly the hunting seat of the dukes of Somerset and later of the earl of Huntingdon, and a mission church dependent on Prestwold.

Burton Overy (8), a large and pleasantly situated village just off the A.6. Several decent houses of 17th- and 18th-century date. The Old Manor House was probably built by John Needham, gent., who bought the manor in 1618. Rectory built c. 1700–10 but added to and spoilt by a later parson. An oak in the garden was planted as a "scion of the Boscobel oak".

The church (St Andrew) is mainly of early 14th-century date, with extensive reconstruction in later Perpendicular period and again in the early 17th century (e.g. south porch, 1618). Some good Perpendicular window tracery, and a good screen (by Leicestershire standards) of the same date.

Just south-west of the church is a field containing earthworks known as "The Banks", gently sloping to a small stream. The origin and purpose of these is not known for certain, but they may well be the remains of the medieval village, deserted possibly at the time of the Black Death.

Cadeby (4) is a small village just south-

east of Market Bosworth. The church (All Saints) is mainly 14th century, remodelled in the Perpendicular style. In the village some timber-framed houses, and also the Manor Farm of early 18th-century date.

Carlton (4), a small village to the north of Market Bosworth and not far from the Ashby-de-la-Zouch Canal, on which it formerly had a wharf. The church (St Andrew) was built of brick in the Classical style in 1764, and was rebuilt in 1867. It is now an ugly Victorian building of no merit. The country round here is pleasant and gently undulating.

Carlton Curlieu (8) is situated high on the western edge of the marlstone escarpment of east Leicestershire, in open and attractive country. Its inhabitants in the 17th century (and probably long before that) were noted for their peculiar manner of speaking. Burton, writing in 1620, says "all those who are born here have an harsh and rattling kind of speech, uttering their words with great difficulty, and wharling in the throat, and cannot well pronounce the letter R". Fuller, later in the 17th century, attributed this "to some occult quality in the elements of the place"; but it was more probably due to the fact that in origin Carlton was a Danish community of free peasants, with their own distinctive speech. By the 18th century this speech was lost and no memory remained of it.

The church (St Mary) and the hall are both notable. A church was founded here probably before the Norman Conquest, and had been given to the Norman Abbey of St Evroul before 1081. This church was rebuilt c. 1150, as is evidenced by the big west tower and the tower arch into the nave. The top stage of the tower was rebuilt in 1686 by Geoffrey Palmer, then squire of Carlton; and a descendant (Sir John Palmer) rebuilt the nave and chancel in 1767. Unfortunately a "restoration" in cheap brick about 1880 destroyed what must have been an interesting Georgian church, if we may judge by the unspoilt church of East Carlton in Northants which was rebuilt by Sir John Palmer about the same time. The interior of Carlton Curlieu is now devoid of interest except for the

Norman tower arch already referred to and a monument to Sir John Bale (d. 1622) and Frances his wife (d. 1624) now hidden away in the vestry.

The Bales built the fine hall just south-east of the church in the 1630s. In the north-west corner of the field in front of the hall is a small rectangular moat where the medieval manor house stood. Carlton Clump is a well-known landmark with views right across country to Charnwood Forest.

Castle Donington (1) is a decayed market town with a good deal of interest, despite the first impression it makes of a shambling untidiness. It was originally called Donington and took its prefix from the castle, the site of which is to be seen—mostly large earthworks—to the north-east of the church. The castle was first built in the 12th century, on the loftiest summit round about, which commanded important crossings of the Trent. The view today over the middle Trent valley must include the largest concentration of pylons in England and is of inconceivable dreariness—the Midlands almost at their worst.

The student of "vernacular building" will find a great deal to interest him in the town, the most notable things being the Key House (1595) and Hall Farm (17th–18th centuries); but the streets should be explored on foot. An excellent study (with map and many attractive old photographs) is J. M. Lee's *The Rise and Fall of a Market Town*, published by the Leicestershire Archaeological and Historical Society in 1956. The intelligent visitor should acquire this, together with another good study by the Castle Donington W.E.A. Group on *The Ancient Kings Mills*, published in 1960, also with map and illustrations. The Kings Mills lie two miles due west of the town, at the foot of a wooded cliff and beside the Trent, in a setting of great beauty. There was an ancient crossing of the Trent from here to Weston-upon-Trent on the Derbyshire side. The mills are recorded in Domesday Book (1086) and have had a continuous history almost to the present day, not only for corn-milling but also for various industrial purposes. There is still much to see here and the visitor should on no account fail

COLD OVERTON Manor

to reach this delightful and historic spot.

The Mills stood on the edge of Donington Park, in which lay Donington Hall, built for the first marquess of Hastings in 1793–5 by Wilkins as what the *Little Guide* calls "a favourable specimen of the Gothic of the time". The Hastings family were ruined by the fourth marquess (1842–68), a jackass of the first order (see the photograph of this ineffable idiot in Lee's booklet). He ran through a great fortune (horses) and by the age of twenty-six was crawling around on a walking-stick. Though the family managed to hang on to the hall amid the financial débacle, it ceased to be a Great House and has since undergone various uses. It is now unoccupied.

Back in the town, the parish church, with its rare dedication to St Edward King and Martyr (murdered in 978) is well worth detailed study. A church stood on this site in 1086—probably soon after Edward's canonisation in 1001—though nothing remains from this early date. The present building was begun *c.* 1200

(see lower part of the tower, the south arcade, and chancel) and enlarged in the 14th century (upper part of tower and spire). The usual clerestory and porch were added in the 15th century. At the west end of the south aisle is the tomb-chest with brasses of Robert Staunton and Agnes his wife. She died in 1458, but the date of his death has never been filled in. In the north aisle is the fine alabaster tomb of Robert Hasylryg (who lived at Donington Park in Henry VIII's time, died 1536) and his wife Eleanor. There is a good detailed guide to the church.

Catthorpe (8), in the most southerly tip of the county, lies huddled between the Roman road Watling Street (now A.5) and the M.1 motorway. Its southern boundary is the Warwickshire Avon, here not far from its source. Those who like to see the infancy of historic rivers can do so by taking the by-road to Lilbourne. The small church (St Thomas) is the usual Leicestershire type, i.e. a building of about 1300 remodelled in the Perpendicular

period, with a rebuilt chancel (19th-century). Note the good 13th-century font, rather like that of All Saints at Leicester.

Chadwell (6) (sometimes known as Caldwell) is only a hamlet at the end of a lane that leads nowhere, in a pretty setting. The little church (St Mary) is charming, with the afternoon sunlight on the decayed golden ironstone, and its rustic interior. It is basically a Norman church, as witness the blocked north arcade showing where an aisle has been demolished, and the Norman font. The square west tower was also built before 1200. The chancel and south aisle are Early English. There was a mild restoration in 1863. Chadwell is best reached from either Scalford or Waltham-on-the-Wolds. Wycombe, another hamlet nearby, has no church, but is worth a stop and an amble round. Both places are recorded in Domesday Book (1086).

Chilcote (1), in the extreme west of the county, was transferred from Derbyshire in 1897. The church (St

Matthew) is a small building in the Gothic style, repaired in 1842 and "thoroughly renovated" in 1885. Before the repairs of 1842 there was a Norman doorway in the north wall of the nave.

Church Langton (8) is the mother-church (St Peter) of a large area around and dominates its countryside. Of ancient foundation, it was largely rebuilt in the Perpendicular style, with a fine lofty interior and good north and south arcades. The south aisle and chancel are, however, early 14th-century (*c.* 1330). Font dated 1662. Fine organ case of *c.* 1760. Note the long series of Kendall headstones in the churchyard, where Ketton stone and Swithland slate are both found.

Church Langton was a rich living and its rectors have included Polydore Vergil, an Italian who resided in England as sub-collector of Peter's Pence 1502–15 (though he never resided at Langton) and Laurence Saunders, martyr, who was burnt to death at Coventry in 1555. Later, the Hanburys were rectors here successively from 1753 to 1899, except for the years 1778–82 when Charles Markham kept the place warm for a young Hanbury. A William Hanbury built the handsome rectory in 1784–6, which Pevsner says "would have been a credit to any affluent nobleman up the river Thames". His father had bought the manor in 1753 and presented himself to the living in the good old way. He founded the Hanbury Trust for a variety of laudable purposes, though some were fantastic. There is a small portrait bust to him in the church (1778).

Claybrooke (7) is really two villages (Magna and Parva), and the parish church (St Peter) is, curiously enough, in Claybrooke Parva. It is a church of altogether lovely proportions, above all the superb chancel of *c.* 1340. Notice especially the flowing Decorated tracery of the windows. The nave and aisles were rebuilt in the latter part of the 15th century, and a clerestory added.

Claybrooke Hall is described as "a large modern mansion" in the 1846 directory. The Fosse Way and Watling Street crossed at the edge of Claybrooke parish, at a point long known as High Cross, originally the major Roman settlement of *Venonae*.

Coalville (4), an unlovely name for an unlovely town which started up on a bleak common when Whitwick Colliery was opened in 1824, at what was then called Long Lane. The Anglicans built Christ Church in 1836–8, and the Baptists their own chapel in 1838. Thereafter the place grew rapidly all through the Victorian decades and is now a town of some 30,000 people. The Clock Tower (1926) is admired by Pevsner. Coalville on a wet day is a gruesome experience: but they make excellent pork pies here as a compensation.

Cold Newton (5) is a much-shrunken village up on the Liassic clays of east Leicestershire, and is rightly named, open as it is to every wind. The country round it is remote and very attractive. It had formerly a small church (now quite gone) and a medieval manor house, the moated site of the latter still clearly visible just east of the road towards the present manor house, which is now a farmhouse of 16th–17th-century date. The earthworks of the former village are most conspicuous to the north of the existing farm buildings and west of the manor house. The site is fully described (with a plan) in my *Seven Deserted Village Sites in Leicestershire* (Leicestershire Archaeological Society, 1956).

Cold Overton (6) stands nearly 700 ft. up on the frontier of Rutland, facing the Siberian winds of an East Midland winter. The spired church (St John the Baptist) is visible from afar: mainly 13th-century, as witness the good Early English arcades, Decorated windows in chancel and south aisle, and the usual Perpendicular clerestory. Some early 14th-century wall paintings in the south aisle, for those who like this sort of thing. The hall is basically a house of 1649–60, built by the St Johns, with a rather grand main staircase "entirely in the Jacobean tradition" (Pevsner).

Coleorton (4) was originally called simply Overton or Orton. The prefix *Cole* was added *c.* 1570 when the coal seams were first vigorously exploited, though there had been earlier mining here as the seams were apparently on fire for many years in the time of Henry VIII. The development of the collieries here in Elizabethan times made the fortunes of the Beaumonts. Coleorton Hall, famous in English literary history, was entirely rebuilt by George Dance the younger in 1804–8 for Sir George Beaumont; the second floor was added by C. R. Cockerell in 1862. Here Sir George, the 7th baronet, entertained Wordsworth, Scott, Coleridge, Southey, Constable, Wilkie, and other notable men of his time. The grounds include a winter garden designed by Wordsworth. The park is still beautifully wooded, though the Beaumonts ceased to live here in 1934 and the hall now belongs to the National Coal Board.

The church (St Mary), close to the hall, is partly Decorated and partly Perpendicular but was much rebuilt in 1851. In the south aisle is a fine monument to Sir Henry Beaumont (d. 1607) and his wife, and a tablet to Sir George Beaumont (d. 1827). In the west window is some Rouen glass of *c.* 1500 brought here by Sir George Beaumont.

The disused railway (opened 1833) and the early coal-mines form an important field for industrial archaeology.

Congerstone (4), a small village near the old Ashby canal. The church (St Mary) is a bit of a mixture, due to the extensive "repairs" by Earl Howe (of Gopsall) from 1834 onwards. The village belonged to the Old English kings, as the name means "king's *tun*".

Copt Oak (4), an ancient cross-roads in the middle of Charnwood Forest, takes its curious name from the "chief oak" at which the ancient Swanimote Court for the manor of Groby met. The original oak was blown down in a gale in 1855. White's *Directory* for 1864 said the roots still remained behind the church. "This is supposed to have been a *Celtic Tau*, the symbol of the Druidical Jupiter, made by cutting away all the branches of the tree but two, which, although separated, were suspended like arms, so as to form a cross. The trunk was 20 ft. high and 24 ft. in circumference."

The church (St Peter) was one of three built to serve the needs of the Forest in 1837. It was "enlarged and beautified" in 1889–90.

Cosby (8) is a pleasantly open village with a stream running through it. There are a number of interesting old houses and barns, including a cruck-framed barn at Church Farm and a 16th-century barn at the Old Hall. The Old Hall itself has 16th-century brickwork with Tudor chimney-stacks. The hearth tax of 1666 shows a village of prosperous free-holders and a number of large farm-houses. The church (St Michael) was poorly "restored" in the 19th century and is uninteresting. But note the nicely lettered slate wall-monument to Richard Miles (1786), an ancient yeoman family in Cosby; the massive medieval oak chest; and the medieval glass in the north nave windows and south chancel windows, apparently pieces of an original 15th-century memorial window to William Bent and Agnes his wife. In the church-yard, see the three remarkably large Swithland slate slabs recording burials of the old yeoman family of Armston continuously from 1633 to 1905. Note, too, the degeneration of the folk-art on memorials between the oldest slab and the latest. The Armstons have almost certainly farmed in Cosby since pre-Conquest times (their name means "son of Orm") and only gave up within recent years. A variant of the name is Armson, which is still well represented in the Leicestershire telephone directory.

Cossington (5), is a pleasant village to find between the red brick messes of Syston and Sileby, having never been industrialised like these two. Cossington Mill, on the Soar, forms an attractive 17th–18th-century group. Many good houses in the village, most notable architecturally being the rectory, c. 1500 in parts at least. The church (All Saints) is partly 13th-century (tower, north arcade, nave) and partly early 14th (chancel, south aisle, south doorway). Fine sedilia in chancel, also some poppy-head stalls.

COLD OVERTON

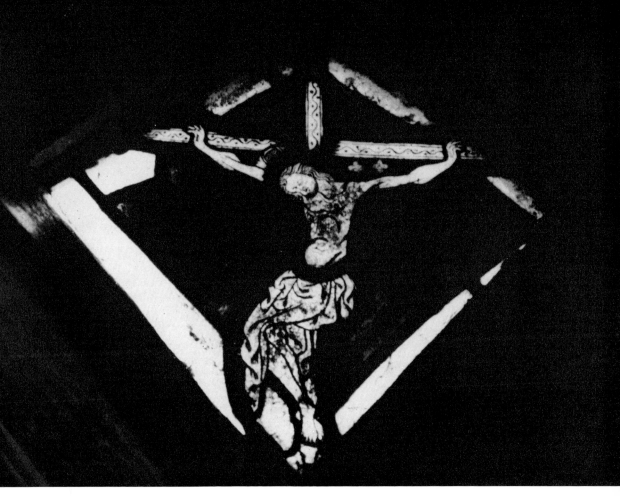

COSTON: the Crucifixion in 14th-century glass

Benches of *c*. 1500 and medieval heraldic tiles.

Coston (6) lies in peaceful and fertile country on the headwaters of the river Eye. Enclosed in the 1630s, the parish characteristically has open, unfenced roads and large fields, orginally pastures. Street Lane, ½ mile north of the village, is an old drovers' road heading for Blue Point on Sewstern Lane: grass-grown, deserted, good walking away from it all.

The church (St Andrew) is mainly of ironstone, with a miniature broach-spire of limestone. Norman window in lower part of tower, but the round-arched north arcade is 13th century; south arcade plain Decorated of

COSTON

14th century. Altogether a pleasant rustic interior. Chancel of 1846, with a good altar-piece of the period. Curious memorial to Temple Crozier, who was "accidentally stabbed on the stage of the Novelty Theatre whilst playing [and] died at his post" on 10 August 1896 aged 24.

Cotes (5), across the river from Loughborough, was once a consider-able village with its own church. There must be a deserted village site round here as very few houses now remain. On the west side of the by-road are the scanty remains of the Old Hall and its large gardens. The Skipwiths bought Cotes in the 1580s and built their house forthwith. Sir Henry Skipwith entertained Charles I here on 28 May 1645. Heavily fined by the Parliamentarians and in debt

to the moneylenders of the City of London, he was obliged to sell out to Christopher Packe in 1650. Sir Christopher (as he soon became) died here in 1682. His grandson Clifton Packe lived here (d. 1707) but in his time the house was almost wholly demolished by fire and was aban-doned by the Packes for their other house at Prestwold (q.v.). The old church also decayed, and in 1846 there were only "some remains" to be seen.

Cotesbach (7) is a small village spoilt by 20th-century building. The church (St Mary) was originally an early 14th-century building, rebuilt in an unusual style in 1812—plain but not unpleasing. Original 15th-century timbers in south porch. The hall of *c*. 1702 was formerly the rectory,

43

IN REMEMBRAN[CE]
OF EDWARD SMI[TH]
ELDEST S[ON] TO
SMITH, AND [OF E]
WIFE, ELDE[ST]
S[ir] EDWARD

built by Edward Wells, rector, and enlarged by his successor, John Fanshawe (1728–63). Dr Wells was a prolific author (26 works listed by Nichols) and a noted mathematician. The manor house, next to the hall, was originally a gabled Jacobean house of 1620–30, much altered in the late 17th century and again in latter part of the 18th century.

Cotesbach was the scene of the great revolt of the Midland peasantry in 1607 against enclosing landlords, but like most revolts in England it came to nothing in the face of the entrenched order.

Countesthorpe (8), on the whole another depressing industrial village with little to commend it. The church (St Andrew) was rebuilt in 1841, except the 15th-century west tower. Southwards, however, the country becomes more attractive and rural.

Cranoe (9) is a small and dwindling village 5 miles north of Market Harborough. The church (St Michael) has a 13th-century west tower, but the rest was rebuilt in 1846–9. The Norman font of an older church remains. Most of the parish has belonged to the Brudenells of Deene (Northants) since Henry VIII's time. The National School is a pleasing little building of 1843.

Croft (7) is a depressing village at the foot of a prominent hill. On this hill Wiglaf, King of Mercia, held a council in the year 836, attended by the archbishop of Canterbury and eleven bishops of the southern province, besides other magnates. The church (St Michael) was thoroughly restored in 1879, and the interior is totally uninteresting. There is, however, a Norman window in the north transept, and the font is a massive late 12th-century affair on a modern base. Medieval stone coffin in churchyard near the south door.

Croxton (pronounced **Cros'n**) **Kerrial** (3) is a large stone-built village high up on the Melton–Grantham road. Round here the outcrop of the Lincolnshire limestone (oolitic) ap-

pears in the villages. There are fine views going north out of the village, at Croxton Banks.

The church (St John the Evangelist) lies on the north edge of the village. The central tower is 15th century as is much of the rest of the church. Inside is the finest collection of late medieval benches (42 in all) in the county, worthy of close study. The altar rails are Laudian, c. 1630–40.

Croxton Park was formerly a hunting-seat of the dukes of Rutland. The house was built c. 1730 by the then duke. The park is nearly 800 acres in area and was the site of the Premonstratensian abbey of Croxton, founded before 1160 and dissolved in 1538. It was bought by the first earl of Rutland (d. 1543) who acquired enormous monastic spoils from Northumberland down to Leicestershire and across to Suffolk and Norfolk. By the 1880s the dukes of Rutland ruled over more than 70,000 acres in seven English counties, a great deal of it monastic plunder (in which they were no worse than the other Tudor magnates and officials). There are no visible remains of the abbey except the fishponds. There was formerly a racecourse in the park, established in the early 19th century.

Dadlington (7) is a tiny village on an eminence above the Ashby-de-la-Zouch Canal. The small church (St James) is mainly rustic work of the mid-14th century. The original timbered roof of the same date survives in the nave and south aisle. In the village, the inn bears the unusual name of the Dog and Hedgehog.

Desford (4), a large village in pleasant country, has a much-restored church (St Martin), with a Perpendicular tower and a Norman font. The Old Hall is a good house of c. 1600. About a mile north is Lindridge, the site of a deserted medieval village and a well-preserved moated (manorhouse) site.

Diseworth (4) was the birthplace of William Lilley, the astrologer, in 1602. White's *Directory* of 1846 is rather severe on him: "He was one of those 'blind buzzards' who first deceive themselves by an assumption

of supernatural powers, and then impose them upon others, by pretending to foretell human events, and to develope the sacred and inscrutable dispensations of Providence." His Almanac was for 36 years as popular as Old Moore's in our time. Many of his predictions were published to please Cromwell and Parliament, who granted him a handsome pension. He died in 1681 and is buried in the church at Walton-upon-Thames.

Diseworth church (St Michael) is mostly late 13th century in date, though there is a Norman window in the chancel. Near the church is a good example of an Elizabethan timber-framed farmhouse.

Langley Priory, about 1½ miles from the village, was founded about 1154 for Benedictine nuns, and dissolved in 1536. Nothing remains of this small foundation. The present "Priory" is basically a house of about 1600, though Pevsner suggests that the wings, especially the north wing, may incorporate medieval work.

Dishley (4), close to the A.6 beyond Loughborough, was once a considerable village but was long ago deserted. It was given to Garendon Abbey (before 1168) who turned it into one large farm (Dishley Grange) which later became the home of Robert Bakewell (1725–95), the celebrated grazier and cattle breeder. Here he produced the famous Leicestershire long-horn cattle and was equally successful with sheep, horses, and pigs. He is buried within the walls of the ruined 13th-century church. Dishley Grange, where he lived, is an attractive Georgian house.

Donington-le-Heath (4) is remarkable for having the oldest medieval house in Leicestershire. It was built from the local Charnwood stone c. 1280 and slightly altered c. 1600. After a period of uncertainty, it was acquired recently by the County Council, who are generously restoring it as one of the most important 13th-century manor houses in England.

Coal was being mined at Donington as early as the 1290s.

Donisthorpe (1), in the messy industrial country round Moira, has a church (St John) built in 1838.

EDMONDTHORPE: Smith monuments

Drayton (9), on the edge of the Welland Valley between Medbourne and Great Easton, used to have its own small Norman church (St James). Nichols, the great historian of Leicestershire, says it had "long been desecrated" even in his time (late 18th century) and "is now converted into a bake-house". A drawing made in 1794 shows a small thatched building with what was evidently once a nave and chancel. In 1878 the remains (the chancel had then gone) were rescued from further desecration by the then owner of Rockingham Castle and restored to proper use for divine service.

Dunton Basset (8) lies on high ground, rising towards the watershed between Trent and Severn (*see* also **Knaptoft** (8)). In the 19th century it was a village largely composed of framework-knitters. The church (All Saints) has a lofty steeple, visible from afar, which was used as a beacon "at the time when Napoleon threatened to invade this kingdom". Basically a church of late 13th–early-14th-century date, but heavily restored in 1882, when the chancel was completely rebuilt. It contains, however, an interesting collection of medieval benches, probably rustic work of the 15th century.

The Duke of Cumberland, the Butcher of Culloden, marched through Dunton on his way north in 1745. Parliament voted him £40,000 a year for life after Culloden, so making him the world's highest-paid butcher. Buried in Westminster Abbey, naturally, in 1765 (he died at the age of 44 by divine providence).

About 1½ miles south-east of Dunton is Cotes de Val, another deserted medieval village with a moated manor house site.

Earl Shilton (7) is a long street village, once full of miserable framework-knitters and now noted for its hosiery and footwear industries. It belonged anciently to the earls of Leicester who built a castle here in the 12th century, of which only the motte remains west of the church. The church (St Simon and St Jude) was described in 1846 as "an old gloomy-looking fabric" and was rebuilt entirely in 1855–6, except the tower. Stencilled walls done by the first vicar, also flowery chancel roof.

East Norton (9), a small village on the main Leicester–Uppingham road, has an ironstone church (All Saints) heavily restored or rebuilt in the middle of the 19th century. Curious south doorway (17th century) and a good 14th-century font. Nice little stone-built house nearby, dated 1643. The country all round here is very hilly and picturesque, worth exploring slowly, in all directions.

Eastwell (3), a small village on the prehistoric road that follows the top of the Wolds for miles, through quiet ironstone country.

The hall is early 17th century (date 1634 on rainwater head), probably built by Rowland Eyre who bought the manor in 1631, with handsome 18th-century stable-block alongside the road. Small Roman Catholic chapel west of the hall, with priest's house attached, built in 1798 in lieu of one formerly in the hall.

The parish church (St Michael) is utterly delightful both outside and in. Small, decayed ironstone mostly. Thin west tower of late 13th century. Nave, chancel, aisles, all of various uneven levels. The humble interior, lit by oil lamps and almost untouched by the restorer, is one of the most appealing country interiors in Leicestershire, or indeed in the East Midlands, and of considerable architectural interest. It is basically 13th century and early 14th, with a clerestory of *c.* 1500; but the astonishing feature is the miniature stone screen between nave and chancel, with a small doorway leading from one to the other. Closer inspection strongly suggests that the chancel was built first (*c.* 1220) and that for some time there was no nave as the massive wall between chancel and nave looks as though it were once an *outside* wall and the doorway an outside door. So the chancel remained a kind of cell. When the nave was added this wall was simply pierced to form a kind of small screen *in situ* and the narrow doorway retained instead of building a normal chancel arch. The south arcade is late 13th-century, the north arcade 15th. In the chancel (north wall) is a well-preserved early 14th-century effigy of a priest holding a chalice, and a mural monument (east wall) to Mrs Patty Faithful (1827), widow of a former rector who, one hopes, was as charming as her name. The chancel roof has rustic, late medieval beams rather like a barn. The Rev. Edward Bullen was rector here for 54 years, dying in 1884 at the age of 89. He was a hunting parson of the old type and is said to have followed the Quorn for 80 years. The cast-iron lectern, an agreeable Victorian affair, was probably put in by him about 1861 when the church underwent a mild restoration.

Eaton (3), an ironstone village high up near the headwaters of the river Devon, in picturesque, broken country. The church (St Denis) is entirely built of ironstone, even the steeple (most unusual this, as ironstone was not usually regarded as resistant enough to the weather). The "pleasing decay" of the fabric is highly photogenic in summer evening light. Mainly a 13th-century building (south and north doorways, and good arcades of same period) with the usual Perpendicular clerestory and roof. Crude chancel screen. Nice slate tablets in chancel. Good views from churchyard.

Edmondthorpe (6), a small village on the frontier of Rutland. The church (St Michael) is large and stately for so small a place. West tower of ironstone (13th century) to which an upper stage of limestone was added in 15th century. The exterior is a pleasing mixture of stones and styles. A nice country interior: I was last here on a January afternoon with the winter rain rustling on the lead roofs, looking at the Smith monuments in the south aisle—a mild English setting that reminded one of Arnold's stanzas on *The Tomb in the Church of Brou*. The interior is mostly Decorated with typical arcades of this period and square-headed windows. Tall plain screen (15th century). Mutilated sedilia in chancel converted into a rustic memorial for an early 18th-century parson, Peter Boundy—a piece of vandalism that time has softened. The Smith monuments: in particular Sir Roger Smith

FOXTON Locks

46

(d. 1655) and his two wives, all recumbent in three tiers. Other Smith memorials down to 1757. They sold the manor in 1762. Their *Hall* now in ruins amid the trees, leaning chimney stacks, hollow rain-washed window openings. A Tudor house much altered about 1700 and again in the late 19th century—a sad memorial to recent English history.

Elmesthorpe (7) is one of the best-marked sites in Leicestershire of a deserted medieval village. It was already deserted in the late 15th-century, so that when Richard III stopped here on his way to the fatal Bosworth Field (August 1485) no accommodation could be found for him, and his officers slept in the church. The church (St Mary) later fell into ruins, but the old chancel was rebuilt in 1868. The nave still lies open to the sky. West tower and font also remain. The line of the former village street is very clearly marked, with the large "platforms" that conceal the foundations of the peasants' houses.

A hundred years ago (White's *Directory*) the parish was "remarkable for its botanical productions, upwards of 90 different plants being sought for here by botanists at the proper seasons for gathering them".

Enderby (7), a large village southwest of Leicester, has little to commend it to the visitor. The church (St John the Baptist) was rebuilt in 1868, except the west tower. The bridge over the Soar, ¾ mile to southeast, is a packhorse bridge probably of 15th-century date. It now stands isolated in a field near Enderby Mill.

Evington (5) is now engulfed by the city of Leicester but retains a little of its former charm. A hundred years ago it was described as "a neat village . . . 275 inhabitants". As late as the 1920s, the *Little Guide* could describe it as "a small and secluded village". It was built around a small green, which survives. Here is the pretty little Gothick chapel of 1837, now used by the Baptists. Evington House was built in 1836, Evington Hall about 1830. The former now belongs to the city and is used as a restaurant, the latter is a convent school. The handsome Cedars Hotel

was for a time the home of the prolific novelist E. Phillips Oppenheim (1866–1946): it became a hotel in 1937.

The church (St Denis) is, like many Leicestershire churches, a building of late 13th–early 14th-century date, restored in 1867 when the chancel was rebuilt and spoilt. The north aisle windows are of excellent 14th-century design: note especially the window in the east wall, and that in west wall. This was probably the Grey aisle: their arms appear in the windows. Some good 18th-century monuments in nave and chancel.

West of the church is a dry moat and a fishpond, remains of the manor house of the Greys, who were lords of Evington from before 1239. The island site is now a playground for children.

Eye Kettleby (6), just west of Melton Mowbray, was once a considerable village, now deserted. The site can be clearly seen between the railway and the main road, running down to the river. The Wreak was formerly called the Eye: hence the odd name of this lost village. There must have been a medieval manor-house here, as the Belers lived here from the 12th to the 15th century. They died out in 1476 and the village was deserted by 1524, if not considerably earlier. A large Elizabethan mansion has similarly disappeared, and so has the little medieval church. This would be a rewarding site to explore.

Fenny Drayton (7) was a tiny village beside the Roman road from Leicester to Watling Street, but has fallen a victim to the commuter-trend and is now heavily bungaloid. George Fox, the founder of the Society of Friends (Quakers) was born here in 1624, the son of a weaver. He is said to have preached his first sermon in this vicinity, under a tree "which was long held in veneration by his followers" who took away so many pieces that it entirely disappeared. The church (St Michael) has a late 12th-century south doorway, but is otherwise mostly 14th century, heavily Victorianised. Chancel of 1860, and much Victorian ironwork and seating. Despite all this, a rather appeal-

ing little interior. The Purefoy monuments run from 1545 to 1628, the earliest being to Nicholas Purefoy and Jane his wife, an alabaster tomb with incised figures charmingly holding hands. A hideous iron safe has been stuck on the top of this tomb with a brutal insensitivity to the past, so characteristic of the present age. Notice the large mural monument to Samuel Bracebridge esquire of Lindley (he built the hall here in 1701) and read his melancholy epitaph. He died 10 November 1736 "after near 40 years Struggle with the *Gout* attended with Exquisite Pain and Torture".

Fleckney (8), a large and dreary industrial village with little to commend it. The church (St Nicholas) is basically Norman in structure, as is shown by the north and south doorways to the nave, but suffered much change and enlargement in 1868–70. Some excellent headstones of Swithland slate in the churchyard, late 18th–early 19th century. The great hosiery firm of Wolsey Ltd. of Leicester may be said to have originated here about 1860, when Robert Walker set up eight stocking frames in a barn at the bottom of the Kibworth road.

Foston (8) is a "lost village" in quiet country south of Leicester. The site of the village, deserted in the 16th century, is marked by earthworks on either side of the by-road leading in from the A.50. The church (St Bartholomew) looks outwardly rather dull, but a Saxon window in the north wall of the nave reveals a pre-Conquest origin for the nave, to which an aisle was added in the 12th century. There was also a south aisle, now blocked, so it was a much larger building altogether round about 1300 when the village flourished. The Faunts, squires of Foston, lived where Hall Farm now stands. Only one memorial to them in the church —Henry Faunt, 1665—which Pevsner calls "bad but engaging".

Foxton (8), a large village of somewhat irregular plan, is a favourite place for Sunday motorists. The

GADDESBY church: the south aisle

48

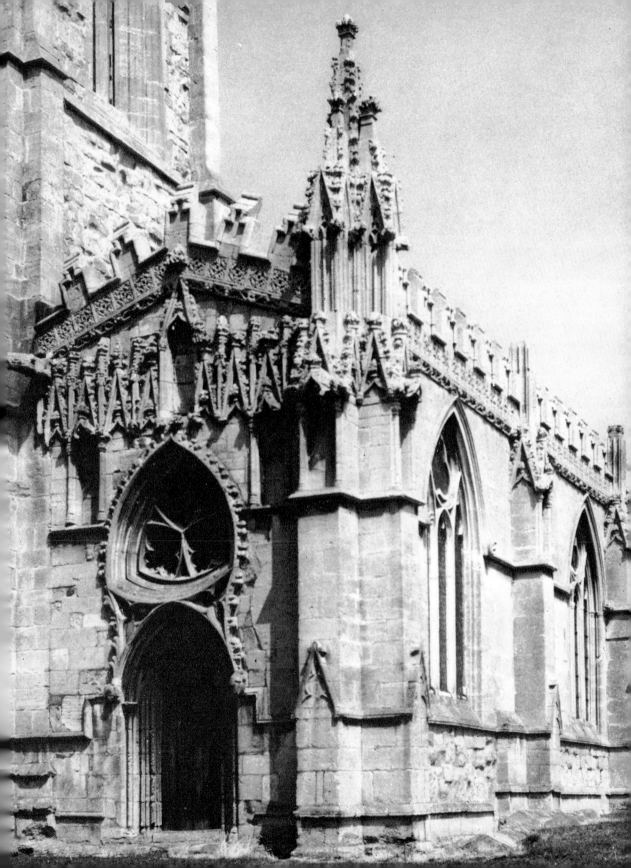

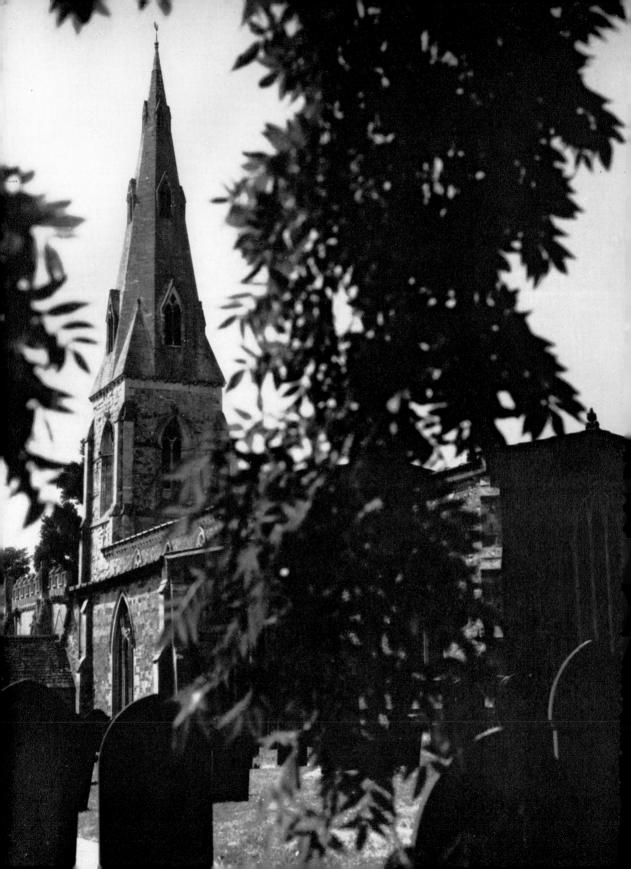

Grand Union Canal here climbs ten locks in succession to reach its summit level: a remarkable piece of canal engineering completed in 1808. In 1900 an inclined plane, 300 ft. long with a rise of 75 ft., was built to replace the locks, but proved too expensive to work and was abandoned in 1911.

The church (St Andrew) is on an ancient site. There was a priest here in 1086 and the existence of part of the shaft of a Saxon cross suggests a pre-Conquest origin for the first church. The present building is the usual Leicestershire peiod—late 13th century to early 14th, with considerable additions and alterations in Perpendicular style (e.g. north aisle windows, clerestory windows, and north arcade). Font, Norman from the older church (c. 1150), but the pedestal is later and made up of two 13th-century capitals from a former arcade.

The manor house, near the church, is possibly medieval in part, much altered and enlarged in 1597.

Freeby (6), a tiny village with a delightful little church (St Mary). The west tower is 15th century, of limestone, but the body of the church is mainly early 14th-century ironstone. Inside, two miniature arcades, the south one particularly pretty with clustered columns. Chancel, 14th-century with late medieval benches. Clerestory added when the tower was built. Font, square with chamfered corners, probably 13th-century.

Frisby (8), a deserted village site in the east Leicestershire uplands nearly 600 ft. up, which is high for Leicestershire. The well-marked site of the old village can be seen immediately south of the Galby–Billesdon by-road. Beautiful pastoral views all round.

Frisby-on-the-Wreak (5) (to distinguish it from Frisby-by-Galby) is a large and attractive village on the south side of the Wreak, which used to be navigable. There are several nice houses, many dated, including the vicarage (1759). The church (St Thomas à Becket) is of various dates: the lower part of the tower is Norman (two windows), the upper part and the spire Decorated work. Chancel, 13th century, and Decorated nave with the usual Perpendicular clerestory. Basically, however, the church is 14th-century, and its most notable feature is the south transept with beautiful south window of c. 1360.

Frolesworth (7). The church (St Nicholas) is again the typical Leicestershire period for rebuilding, i.e. late 13th century to early 14th, with a Perpendicular clerestory. The chancel was rebuilt when the clerestory was added. So, too, was the tower, but the top is a further rebuilding of 1762. Altar-tomb with effigy of Francis Staresmore (d. 1626); tomb of his wife erected 1658. The nice 18th-century almshouses occupy three sides of a square, founded in 1725 by Rt. Hon. John Smith, Lord Chief Baron of the Exchequer in Scotland. Added to in 1760, 1796, and 1834. Smith was born at Frolesworth in 1656.

Gaddesby (5) has one of the most striking and beautiful medieval churches in the Midlands, certainly

GADDESBY, *below left* medieval benches; *below right* the Cheney monument

among villages. It is notable both as a building and for its contents. Dedicated to St Luke, the present church dates from *c.* 1240 to *c.* 1340 and bears few marks of later restoration. The south aisle was begun in the second quarter of the 13th century (cf. the south doorway) and proceeded from east to west, being completed about 1300. The embattled parapet and rich canopy work were added 1330–40. The sudden ending of this beautiful work may be attributable to the Black Death. The north aisle, begun about the same date, was beautified in the 14th century, but not to the same degree as the other aisle. The chancel was rebuilt in the 15th century. The clerestory, which completes the lofty nave, is 14th century in date—unusually early in Leicestershire where most clerestories are a century later.

There are 18 medieval benches, but note also the stone seating round the bases of the piers and along the walls, and the panelled box-pews. Note, too, the sculptured heads of the south aisle windows (external), the fine medieval altar-tombs, and the Decorated font. The extraordinary memorial to Col. Cheney (d. 1848) is, as Pevsner says, "more suited for St Paul's Cathedral than for a village church". Col. Cheney lived at Packe Hall nearby (now called Gaddesby Hall). He fought at Waterloo: four horses were killed under him that day.

Galby (8), a small village on the summit of the Marlstone uplands in beautiful, unspoilt country. The church (St Peter) has a striking 18th-century tower and nave—all rebuilt in 1741 except the chancel (early 16th-century). Built by the elder Wing whose son built King's Norton (q.v.), a much more sophisticated piece of work. Galby church was restored in 1960. It is always open and is now an appealing village church well worth a visit.

Garendon (4) was a Cistercian abbey founded in October 1133 and dissolved in 1536. The site was granted to the Earl of Rutland, one of the largest beneficiaries in the wholesale plunder that followed the Dissolution of the Monasteries. It was sold to Sir Ambrose Phillipps in 1683 and

a grand early Georgian house was erected on the site. This is described in Pevsner's *Leicestershire and Rutland (q.v.)* but has been destroyed (in 1964) since he wrote. The M.1 motorway thunders over the precise site. There was almost certainly a village here before the Cistercians took over. The changes at Garendon during the last 900 years would make a nice study in landscape history.

Garthorpe (6) has a pretty little church (St Mary), mainly built in the 13th and 14th centuries of local ironstone, and altered and enlarged in Lincolnshire limestone in the Perpendicular period. The attractive west tower belongs to this period. The south arcade has round arches of early 13th-century date, the north arcade about 1300. Easter sepulchre and aumbry in the chancel. Some fragments of early 14th-century glass in north aisle (west and east windows). The tiny village stands on the upper reaches of the river Eye. Its old corn mill was still working in 1928, but is now gone.

Gilmorton (8), a large village near the source of the river Swift nearly 500 ft. above sea-level, which is high for Leicestershire. The church (All Saints) was rebuilt in 1860 (except the tower) and is dark and dull, but connoisseurs of the mid-Victorian may find the costly fittings worthy of study. The large earthwork immediately west of the church is probably the site of a moated manor house.

Glenfield (5), now largely overrun by Leicester, had a 13th-century church (now in ruins) which was replaced in 1877 (St Peter). A 15th-century effigy of a lady was transferred from the old church to the new. Glenfield tunnel (1830–32) on the old Leicester–Swannington Railway, 1 mile 36 yds. long, was the longest tunnel in England at the time.

Glen Parva (8), now swallowed up in the subtopian sprawl between Wigston and Blaby, retains a small timbered manor house of late medieval date, somewhat altered in the 19th century. At Glen Hill an important Anglo-Saxon burial ground (6th-century) was unearthed about 100 years ago.

Glooston (9), a small village in a hollow, was occupied in Roman times. The site of a villa—the Romano–British equivalent of a country house and estate—was found in 1946 on the east bank of the stream. The Gartree Road (Roman) runs just south of the village. At the west end of the village is the moated site of a medieval manor house.

The church (St John the Baptist) was founded in the 12th century, but is now largely a rebuilding of 1866–7, retaining only a piscina and font from the medieval church. The manor was bought by the Brudenells of Deene in 1632 and still belongs to them. Attractive unspoilt country all round here.

Goadby (9). The church (St John the Baptist) has a western bellcote instead of a tower. Nave and chancel all one: ironstone of the 13th century. The south porch retains its timbered medieval roof; south door is dated 1618. Goadby church was founded as a manorial chapel in the 12th century. Home Farm, immediately south of church, is an ironstone house of 1680, a time of great prosperity for big Leicestershire graziers. The attractive "Victorian Tudor" building nearby was built as the National School in 1857.

Goadby Marwood (6), remote in the north Leicestershire wolds. The church (St Denis) is attractive: mainly built round about 1300 (see the north and south arcades) with a good and well-kept interior. Beautiful Decorated tracery in south aisle, and good font of this date, too. Some medieval glass in west window and late medieval benches in chancel. The church is "typical" Leicestershire, i.e. built in late 13th-early 14th century, with a Perpendicular clerestory added. Still lit by oil.

Francis Peck, the antiquary, was rector here 1723–43 and is buried in the south aisle. George Villiers, later Duke of Buckingham, spent his early years chiefly at Goadby Hall, a handsome ironstone house in a small park.

Gopsall (1) was originally a village

GALBY:
Chinese taste, 1741

52

with its own church, all gone long ago. So, too, has the magnificent Georgian house that crowned the "gentle eminence" from the 1750s onwards, in a deer-park that stretched over a thousand acres at its greatest extent early in this century. The house was built for Charles Jennens, descendant of Humphrey Jennens, a wealthy Birmingham iron-master who had bought the estate in 1685. Charles Jennens was known in his time as "Solyman the Magnificent" and his house, designed by John Westley of Leicester, cost over £100,000—perhaps equal to a million today. This house was demolished in 1951, but the Entrance Lodge by Wyattville, an adaptation of the Arch of Constantine, still stands near Twycross village. A stone obelisk, originally erected by Pope at Twickenham to the memory of his mother, formerly stood near the house, but was removed by Earl Howe at the demolition of Gopsall to his grounds at Penn in Buckinghamshire. Handel was a close friend of Charles Jennens and composed part of the "Messiah" and "Israel in Egypt" at Gopsall. The Howes sold Gopsall to Sir Samuel (later Lord) Waring, the furniture magnate. King Edward VII was a frequent visitor in the shooting season.

Grace Dieu (4), beside the Loughborough–Ashby road, was a priory for Augustinian nuns founded c. 1239 and dissolved by the rapacious Henry VIII in 1538. In 1539 the site was acquired by John Beaumont, a Tudor lawyer who became Master of the Rolls in 1550. He was "deprived of his offices and fined for grossly abusing his position for his own advantage" in 1552. He converted part of the priory buildings into a residence, so that the few remaining ruins are partly medieval but chiefly domestic Tudor (e.g. fireplaces and chimney-stacks). Grace Dieu Manor, a little to the south in a small park, was built for Ambrose Phillipps de Lisle in 1833–4. He was the most important patron of Catholicism in Leicestershire in the days of its 19th-century revival.

Great Bowden (9), a large village near Market Harborough, of which it was the mother-village. The church (St Peter and St Paul) stands on a very ancient site, but nothing of the present building is older than the second half of the 13th century. Basically it is c. 1280–1350, with considerable alterations and additions in the 15th century (e.g. the north chapel and the clerestories). The memorials include a small brass to a medieval rector (1403), a large marble tablet (signed J. Wing) to Henry Shuttleworth and his two wives, and a tablet to York Powell, Regius Professor of Modern History at Oxford (d. 1904).

There is a large green and the village retains many attractive old houses, including Tudor House (probably medieval in origin) and the Old Rectory (mainly late 17th century). The Old Bakery also has 16th-century work.

Great Dalby (6) lies in a green hollow in the hills, and is chiefly remarkable for its curiously attractive church (St Swithin). The medieval steeple crashed down in 1658, wrecking the nave, which was then rebuilt in a 17th-century version of Gothic. The tower and chancel are what was left of the medieval church. The country to the south is rolling, quiet, and remote.

Great Easton (9), a large village on the edge of the Welland valley, contains many pleasing old houses of 16th–18th-century date and is worth exploring on foot. There is evidence for the existence of a Romano–British building south-west of the church. The latter (St Andrew) is a daughter-church of Bringhurst on its hill about 2 miles off (q.v.), but even so retains some traces of Norman masonry in the north wall. Good west tower of late 13th century, with a bold broach spire. The rest of the church is 13th–14th century, with the usual Perpendicular alterations. Pulpit Jacobean. The church plate includes a paten of c. 1350, the oldest piece in the county.

Great Glen (8) is a large village with some attractive 18th- and early 19th-century houses in the older part. The church (St Cuthbert) was described in a directory of 1863 as "once a goodly structure in the Decorated style . . . much in need of a thorough restoration". Dread words: in 1876 the church had the "thorough restoration" and was pretty well ruined as a result. A Norman south doorway survives, however, and two sculptured stones of pre-Conquest date are to be found in the vestry, and a third above the north doorway. The 14th-century west tower escaped the restoration. There was evidently a church here in pre-Conquest times. A royal charter was issued from Glen in the year 849.

Great Stretton (8) lies on the Roman road, later called the Gartree road. The village is now deserted, though the site and that of the moated manor house are to be clearly seen in the field south of the church. The latter (St Giles) now stands alone, an appealing little building despite a mixed restoration in 1838, with odd bits of medieval masonry built into the walls of the nave. The south doorway is probably Norman, the font Decorated (early 14th century). The low west tower is Perpendicular with some 17th-century repair. Most of the clear glass windows date from 1838; so do the plain box-pews. In spite of all this tampering, Great Stretton is an atmospheric little church to visit on a winter afternoon.

Grimston (5) is a small village on the southern slopes of the Leicestershire Wolds. The church (St John) is mostly 13th century in date but the general effect is Perpendicular because of the windows. The interior is of little interest, but the worn and lumpy ironstone of the exterior is, as always with ancient ironstone, more pleasing.

Groby (4) (pronounced Grooby) is a dull village on the whole, but has a few interesting things in and near it. Most noted of these is Groby Pool, a natural pool 38 acres in extent which is said to have been formerly nearly twice that size. Leicester Abbey had the right of fishing "in the great pool of Groby" on the eve of the four festivals of the Virgin Mary, a privilege which they probably obtained from their founder, Robert le Bossu, second earl of Leicester, in 1143. As the largest natural sheet of water in the county,

GREAT DALBY

it attracts great numbers of winter birds.

Little remains of Groby Castle, one of the many strongholds of the earls of Leicester, except the artificial mount. Erected during the turbulent reign of Stephen, the castle was demolished as long ago as 1176. Near this site is the old Manor House, once the seat of the Greys before they built Bradgate (*q.v.*). The older parts are of stone (probably early 15th century); the brick parts are the work of the Greys *c.* 1485–90.

The church was built in 1840 "in the Norman style". There are syenite (granite) quarries at Groby, and formerly a slate quarry.

Gumley (8) is a pleasant village high on a small but conspicuous range of hills. It must be a site of considerable antiquity as the Mercian King Aethelbald held a council here in the year 749 at which he issued a charter to the churches of his kingdom, freeing them from all public burdens except the fundamental duties of repairing bridges and maintaining fortresses. Gumley church (St Helen) may therefore occupy a very old site—it is noteworthy that St Helen was the mother of the emperor Constantine the Great—but the present building is mostly a good restoration of 1875, except the 14th-century western tower and spire.

Nevertheless, it makes a pleasant grouping on a hillock amid trees. Gumley Hall (1764) has been demolished, but the beautiful woods and the lake remain.

Hallaton (9) is a large and attractive village amid some of the pleasantest hill-country of east Leicestershire. There are several good houses of 17th–early 19th-century date. The *Old Royal Oak* inn was formerly the *Angel* and changed its medieval name presumably at the Restoration. Much rebuilt, but parts appear to be Elizabethan in date.

The church (St Michael) is one of the finest village churches in the county, with an imposing west tower (probably Norman, refaced in the 13th century) surmounted by a good broach-spire which is not, however, in the same class as Market Harborough. Externally, too, the enriched north aisle (built 1330–40) is notable, above all the beautiful Decorated turret at the north-east end made to contain stone images. Internally, the north arcade is late 12th century (except the first arch, which is a 13th-century extension). The south arcade was rebuilt in the 13th century, as was the chancel with its sedilia and piscina. The font is of the same date. In the porch is a dramatic tympanum preserved from the Norman church.

A little west of the village, and well worth visiting, are the earthworks of a considerable "adulterine" (i.e. unlicensed) castle probably constructed in the civil wars of Stephen's reign (1135–54) to protect the iron-working site nearby. This is clearly evidenced by the broken nature of the ground near the castle. The castle probably had a timber keep: no traces of stone buildings have been found.

Hamilton (5) is a good example of a deserted village site, long marked on the Ordnance map as "Town of Hamilton", a mystifying reference. It formerly had a small manor house, a church, and about ten peasant houses, and was deserted and given over to cattle and sheep pastures about the middle of the 15th century. It is a very clearly marked site, especially in winter and early spring before the grass obscures the earthworks. A little to the north-east,

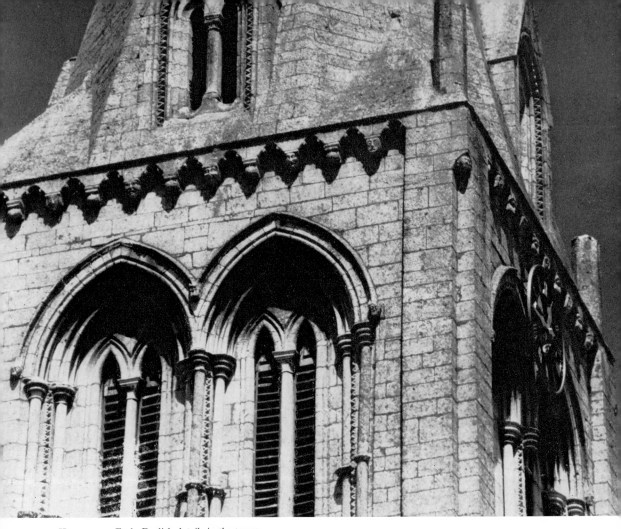

HALLATON: Early English details in the tower

near the footpath to Beeby, is the site of a Roman villa which has never been excavated. Quantities of *tesserae* and pottery have been found here.

Harby (3) is a considerable village in the Vale of Belvoir. The Nottingham–Grantham Canal, opened in 1793, closed in 1929, passes near by. Formerly a wharf here, and a large granary (1836) still stands by the canal. The church (St Mary) is mostly 14th century, of ironstone, restored in 1870–6.

The road up to Waltham-on-the-Wolds is an old drovers' road: hence the great width of the grass verges in places. It may well be prehistoric in origin.

Harston (3). The name means "grey stone", probably referring to a boundary stone where the counties of Leicestershire and Lincolnshire met along the ancient road called Sewstern Lane or The Drift. This is another drove-road, probably continuously used since the Bronze Age, joining the Trent to the Welland across high ground. Some good away-from-it-all walking along the Drift between the Denton road and Brewer's Grave, with views over the Devon valley to Belvoir Castle.

Considerable iron-working round here has revealed Iron Age pits and Anglo-Saxon (5th-century) pit-dwellings, possibly denoting continuous occupation of this upland since pre-Roman times. The church (St Michael) has a 14th-century west tower, but the rest was heavily restored in 1871–88. In the east wall is an Anglo-Saxon carved stone, perhaps part of a 10th-century cross-shaft.

Hathern (4), a large village mostly just off the teeming A.6, with a church (St Peter and St Paul) that was massively restored and rebuilt in 1861–2 as a memorial (alas!) to a beloved Victorian vicar. It was formerly a village of framework-knitters, a domestic industry which lingered on well into the present century. Zouch Bridge, over the Soar, was called *Sottesbrigge* in the late 13th century: the present bridge dates from 1793.

Heather (4) (pronounced Heether), a small village overlooking the Sence valley, has a church (St John the Baptist) that was heavily restored at various dates in the 19th century. Mural monument in chancel to Stephen Everard, 1615.

Hemington (1) has a ruined church, mainly 1300–30. Tower 13th century, with a stumpy broach spire added early 14th century. As long ago as 1589 it was recorded as "a fair church, but the glass all ruined [Elizabethan vandals, an old complaint] and the church not in use to that end it was builded". Leicester Abbey owned the church, which

probably ceased to be served when the abbey was dissolved in 1539 and the rectory fell into lay hands.

Remains of a medieval house west of the church. Some interesting timber-framed houses in the village.

Higham-on-the-Hill (7) stands on an isolated hill as the name implies. The church (St Peter) is interesting despite being terribly over-restored. The west tower is early/Norman, and was probably once a central tower, the western part of the church having been demolished. It stands on a little plateau with wide views over south-west Leicestershire.

Hinckley (7) is a prosperous industrial town, with little for the visitor to enthuse over. As the two great Leicester-

shire industries—hosiery and boots and shoes—expanded rapidly in the late 19th and early 20th centuries—much of the town is dull red-brick streets. Even the large church (St Mary) is disappointing, mostly early 14th century, with considerable additions and changes in the 1870s. There are, however, some amusing medieval corbels in the nave, stone faces which one suspects might be contemporary portraits.

The Unitarian chapel (Great Meeting), off Bond Street, is dated 1722, and there are a few old houses worth looking for. Of the former castle, nothing but the motte survives.

Hoby (5) is built on a bluff overlooking the peaceful Wreak valley. The village contains several timber-

HALLATON

57

framed buildings, including at least one good example of a "cruck" cottage. The church (All Saints) is a bold affair, mostly of ironstone and nearly all *c.* 1300 except the Perpendicular clerestory. Several late medieval benches, screen with some old work, and a medieval stone altar in the south aisle.

Holwell (6) is a tiny village at the head of a valley in the Leicestershire Wolds. Ironstone has been worked here for the iron ore since the 1870s. The small church (dedication unknown) is also of ironstone, built about 1300, with a later bell-cote.

Holyoak (9), now represented by a single farm overlooking the Eye Brook Reservoir, was formerly a village. It probably disappeared before 1600 as William Burton does not mention it in his *Description of Leicestershire* (1622). The site of the village may now lie under the water.

Horninghold (9), is a most attractive "estate village", mostly dating from the early part of this century, in a beautiful setting. The church (St Peter) is also of great interest, having been very conservatively restored. Perhaps I could quote my own words, written 20 or so years ago and still happily true: "it illustrates so well the typical development of the simple English country church growing around its original Norman nucleus, each century seeing some addition,

large or small, to the fabric". Its development is as follows: first a small Norman church of nave, chancel, and west tower built *c.* 1150, of which the south doorway is now the most obvious sign. A south aisle was added early in the 13th century (*c.* 1220) and a north aisle in the latter part of the same century, apparently in two stages. The broach spire was added to the tower *c.* 1300. In the 15th century, as so often in Leicestershire, a clerestory was added to the nave and a new roof inserted. New seating was also provided, of which a few poppy-head bench-ends survive. Some new windows were inserted at the same time. The altar rails are 18th century. Altogether this is a highly atmospheric village church, well worth a special pilgrimage.

Hose (3), like many villages in the Vale of Belvoir, has a rather complicated ground-plan (see Harby and Long Clawson also). The name comes from the Old English *hohas*, "hills", and refers to the prominent escarpment of the Leicestershire Wolds to the south. The Grantham–Nottingham Canal (1793) cuts through the parish and formerly had a wharf here. The church (St Michael) is mostly of ironstone, with a very large ashlar limestone clerestory of 16th-century date. Externally the church is an attractive mixture of stones and styles, with some old brick also. West tower of 14th-cen-

tury, with the usual upper stage added *c.* 1500. Interior mainly early 14th-century with a large rustic font.

Hoton (5) has several timber-framed houses of 16th–17th-century date, and some good Georgian brick houses. The church (St Leonard) has a west tower of early 16th-century date: all the rest rebuilt 1838 and of no interest.

Houghton-on-the-Hill (5) stands high (hence its name of "hill village") just off the Leicester–Uppingham road, its long winding main street being determined by the underlying gravel ridge. The old village near the church has many good 18th-century brick houses. It was the ancestral home of the Herricks, who take their name from a Scandinavian Erik in pre-Conquest days. Tobias Herrick was rector here 1605–27 and Abigail Herrick, mother of Dean Swift, is said to have been born here.

The church (St Catherine) is mostly 14th century in date: the solid west tower is *c.* 1360. North arcade *c.* 1330, south arcade *c.* 1400. Unrestored south porch with original timbers in roof. Consecration crosses on west face of tower near south corner. An ancient stone built in at the foot of the east wall of the south porch is said to have the date of an earlier church on it: MXIV (1014).

Hugglescote (4) is as unlovely as its name. The old church (St John the

Baptist) was demolished in 1878 and replaced by what we now see.

Humberstone (5) is now completely engulfed in the conurbation of Leicester, but a few interesting old houses remain near the church.

The church (St Mary) retains its 14th-century west tower, but the rest was rebuilt in 1858. Despite this unpromising date, Jack Simmons's guide to Leicester roundly says that "anybody who thinks he dislikes Victorian church-work should go to Humberstone: if he has an open mind, he will hardly be able to escape its fascination. All the carved work is elaborate and well executed. Much of it is in alabaster, a material that is rarely used, as it is here, for fonts and the capitals of pillars. Notice the

delicate carving of the foliage in the nave, which has caught something of the spirit of the medieval craftsmen. In the chancel a pretty series of small panels runs round the wall, mounted in terracotta; and on the north wall is an interesting monument commemorating members of the Paget family, especially Thomas Paget (1778–1862), M.P. for Leicester at the passing of the great Reform Act." In the north aisle is an incised alabaster slab to Richard Hotoft, 1451. On the north side of the chancel is a memorial window to the Rev. John Dudley who was vicar here for no less than 62 years. His father and grandfather had held the living for 80 years before him, so the Dudleys ruled here for 142 years between them, down to 1856.

Huncote (7) is a considerable village just north-east of the prominent Croft Hill, in which there are large quarries of syenite. It anciently had a church, said to have been ruined as far back as 1622. The present church (St James) was built in 1898.

Hungerton (5) is a pleasant village with many dated brick houses between 1766 and 1775. A monument in the church to Shuckburgh Ashby (1792, by Thomas Banks) tells us that "he almost wholly rebuilt [the village] from a principle laudable and truly disinterested . . ." The village retains a delightful quiet Georgian air.

The church (St John) is mostly Decorated Gothic, early 14th-century. Chromatic decoration outside

KEGWORTH: vernacular building

with bands of ironstone and limestone, the two commonest building
stones in all of east Leicestershire.
Norman font (apparently now up-
side down), 15th-century parclose
screen cutting off the south aisle,
which formed the private preserve
of the Ashbys of Quenby (*q.v.*).
Monuments to the Ashbys 17th–
18th centuries. George Ashby (1724–
1808) was rector of Hungerton 1754–
67 and became President of St Johns
College, Cambridge, whence he
retired in 1775 to a living in deep-
est Suffolk—a typical 18th-century
career of its kind. One need hardly
add that he was a notable antiquary.

Husbands Bosworth (8) gets its odd
name to distinguish it from Market
Bosworth some miles away. It was
the "farmers' Bosworth" while the

other was a market town. It stands
high on the south border of Leicestershire, and is worth walking round for
its nice old brick houses, including a
Baptist chapel of 1807. The church
(All Saints) was largely rebuilt in
1861–7, but retained a good west
tower and spire of 14th-century date.

Ibstock (4) is a large coal-mining and
industrial village. The church (St
Denis) is all early 14th century, the
vicarage Georgian.

Illston-on-the-Hill (8) stands nearly
600 ft. above sea-level (very high for
Leicestershire) in unspoilt country.
The village was once much larger
and continued southwards from the
present end of the street. There are
clear indications of former house
sites in the field into which the main

street disappears, including a prominent windmill mound. The manor
house was built *c.* 1590 in ironstone
and enlarged in brick 1794. Arms
over the front door with motto "*In
parvo quies*".

The church (St Michael) is mainly
early 14th century, over-restored in
1866. Early 13th-century font, fine
sedilia and piscina of early 14th
century. Monuments to the Need-
hams, who lived in this peaceful spot
from 1588 onwards.

Ingarsby (5), about 1½ miles north of
Houghton-on-the-Hill, is a "lost
village", the best site of its kind in
the county. It was finally depopulated by Leicester Abbey (who
owned the manor) in 1469. The
entire plan of streets, lanes, and
house sites can be clearly traced,
especially in winter or early spring
before the grass is fully grown.
Ingarsby Old Hall has a late 15th-
century wing which was probably
built *c.* 1470 as the bailiff's house for
the monastic estate. The Caves
acquired the site, with much else,
and seem to have enlarged the house
in Elizabethan times (1579). The
house was refronted *c.* 1706. Beautiful quiet green country all around
here.

Isley Walton (4), a chapelry in the
parish of Kegworth. The small
church (All Saints) was built in 1819
but retains a Georgian font, presumably from an older building.

Kegworth (1) is a large village with
several interesting examples of what
is now called "vernacular architecture", i.e. native building, including
much dating from the days when it
was a manufacturing village full of
framework-knitters. It formerly had
a weekly market and four annual
fairs, four corn-mills, a large brewery
and four malthouses, "two excellent
boarding schools, and many well-
stocked shops". It was, in fact, a
small and flourishing country town,
with a brisk canal trade as well as by
road. Kegworth Bridge spans the
river Soar and the Grand Union
Canal, which meet here, and was the
site of a large wharf.

KINGS NORTON church

60

KEGWORTH: Framework knitters' workshop, c. 1840

The church (St Andrew) is "a large and almost faultless village church . . . built, with the exception of the lower part of the tower, at one style, the late Decorated". The tower is mostly early 13th century, rising to early 14th in the upper stages, and so to an elegant recessed spire. Though the nave and chancel look clearly early 14th century in build, there is good evidence for saying that the whole church was built at the expense of Sir Henry Greene, a successful judge, who bought the two manors in Kegworth by 1354. He died in 1369. Work may well have begun earlier than 1354, however, and anyway one must allow for conservatism in styles, not to say the age of the local master-mason. The clerestory was added early in the 15th century. The walls have been scraped of their plaster, like so many other churches in the county. There is a magnificent Royal Arms in the correct position over the chancel arch, carved in high relief, and dated 1684—twenty years earlier than that at Lockington which it resembles.

Keyham (5) is a pleasant village with a much-restored Perpendicular church but still attractive in a homely way. The historian Nichols writes c. 1800: "In this sequestered spot is a boarding-school for young ladies,

under the superintendence of a very respectable lady, Miss Woodford. The number of boarders is between 50 and 60; who on Sunday make a very pleasing appearance at church among the rustic worshippers. They occupy the chancel, where they appear like beds of lilies in a flower garden."

Keythorpe (9) is a "lost village", the site being marked on the map as Old Keythorpe. It was depopulated for sheep pastures about 1450. The hall is a bold-fronted Georgian house on rising ground, "built in the Roman style" in 1843 from Tilton stone.

Kibworth (8) consists of two villages —Kibworth Beauchamp and Kibworth Harcourt. At the latter is a 12th-century castle mound, and several good brick-built Queen Anne and Georgian farmhouses. A beautiful house dated 1678 is said to have been the home, for a time, of Dr Philip Doddridge (1702–51), the eminent Nonconformist divine who was minister at Kibworth in 1723–9. A Congregational meeting-house, built in 1759, still stands at the north end of the village. The parish church (St Wilfred) is large and handsome, mostly Decorated work of the early 14th century, but the tower is 1832–6 having been rebuilt after the spire

fell. Excellent corbel heads in north and south aisles. Good sedilia. Screen much restored.

The neighbouring village of Kibworth Beauchamp has a number of nice houses dating from the 16th century to the 19th.

Kilby (8) has a rebuilt church (St Mary Magdalen, 1858). Extensive moated site in field near the stream, formerly the medieval manor house. At Kilby Bridge (over the Grand Union Canal) is a small canal settlement dating from 1793.

Kimcote (8). The church (All Saints) is partly late 13th century, partly early 14th. Font dated 1654. Free School built 1844. Great Poultney Farm, about 1 mile south-south-west marks the site of the deserted village of Poultney, depopulated in the late 15th century. It can be reached by a footpath beginning near the church.

Kings Norton (8), on the edge of the east Leicestershire hill-country, has one of the most appealing village churches in the Midlands—almost cathedral-like as one first sees it across the fields. Built in 1757–75 by a Leicester architect (John Wing the younger) it is, says Nikolaus Pevsner, "of the churches of the Early Gothic Revival . . . one of the most remarkable in England". Inside all is clear light and serenity. The church (St John the Baptist) has also been called "a perfect expression of 18th-century Anglicanism" retaining its original fittings without change, above all the beautiful three-decker pulpit, the box-pews, and the west gallery. The font is, however, later (after 1850 when the spire fell and crushed it).

Close to the church is the old manor house of the Fortreys, who paid for the rebuilding of both Kings Norton and Galby (1741), a house probably built in the time of James I or Charles I by the Whalleys. Near by is a brick dove-cote of late 17th-century date.

Kirby Bellars (5), standing by the winding river Wreak, has a striking church (St Peter), remarkable both for its isolated position and its size. The name suggests that a church already stood here in pre-Conquest times: its apparent isolation is due to the fact that the original village disappeared centuries ago: and its beauty and size to the fact that it was made a collegiate church in 1315 and became a priory church in 1359.

The Augustinian priory buildings lay to the north of the church, where earthworks may be seen in the field. An even larger area of earthworks, resembling a golf-course for beginners, lies between the railway and the main road at Kirby Park. The whole site is rather confusing, but would seem to contain the earthworks of the "lost village" and possibly the fish-ponds, etc., of the priory. The priory was dissolved in 1536. The site passed into secular hands, and on part of it an ironstone manor house was built, now known as Kirby Park. In the early 19th century this became the hunting-box of Sir Francis Burdett (1770–1844), politician and social reformer, who finished up, however, as a Tory M.P. Kirby Gate, close by, is one of the Holy Places of Hunting, being the traditional scene for the opening meet of the Quorn.

The church has a noble west tower and broach spire, of the usual decayed ironstone with limestone dressings. The south arcade is Early English, the pillars having detached shafts. The north arcade has been

demolished, so there is no north aisle today. Chancel screen: 15th-century. Two alabaster effigies in a recess *c.* 1360 of a knight and his lady. A lofty, dignified interior altogether, on an ancient site. I suspect Kirby has Roman origins: the road running due east–west from Kirby Gate towards Stapleford Park and beyond is almost certainly Roman, and pottery, etc., of that period has been found in a corner of Kirby churchyard.

KIRBY MUXLOE castle

Kirby Muxloe (4) is notable for its magnificent brick-built castle, built in 1480–4 for William, Lord Hastings, who was beheaded in June 1483. The work was therefore hastily brought to a close. There was a 14th-century manor house on the site, of which the basic plan is marked out on the lawn within the restored castle quadrangle. Surrounded by a moat about 120 yds. by 100 yds., and fitted with gun-ports, Kirby Muxloe was intended to be (like Hastings's principal residence at Ashby-de-la-Zouch, *q.v.*) a great man's fortified stronghold at a time of civil war and near-anarchy in England. The castle fell into ruin. Only the great gatehouse and one of the four angle-towers remain impressive, but the whole has been well restored by the Ministry of Works and there is a good printed guide available on the site.

Kirby Muxloe village has now become suburbanised and the church is mostly a rebuilding of 1858. But the castle is worth going a long way to see.

Kirkby Mallory (7) lies directly on the Roman road from Leicester to Mancetter (*Manduessedum*), but the line is lost through the park of Kirkby Hall. It is preserved in the road back to Peckleton and beyond. A church must have stood here before the Norman Conquest, but the present building (All Saints) is mostly 14th century, much modified later. The north aisle, for example, was demolished in the 18th century. Various Noel monuments, especially Sir William Noel (1679). The daughter of Lord Byron (Ada Augusta Lovelace, d. 1852) is buried in the churchyard. Her mother, Lady Byron, lived at the Hall and is described in White's *Directory* for 1846 as "relict of that highly popular poet, the late Lord Byron". Byron had married the Noel heiress in 1815.

Kirkby Moats, about 1 mile north of the village, is of unknown origin, but may be associated with Kirkby Old Parks, a little further north. If so, it probably represents the site of the medieval manor house and its adjacent hunting-park.

Knaptoft (8), a "lost village" and a ruined church, lies just off the A.50, which was the principal medieval road between Leicester and Northampton. It also lies, rather surprisingly, on one of the great watersheds of England, for streams rising in the parish flow to the Soar and hence to the Trent and the North Sea, and to the Avon and so to the Severn and the Bristol Channel. Another stream reaches the Welland, and thence the Wash.

Knaptoft was depopulated and turned into sheep and cattle pastures in the late 15th century by the Turpins, whose hall, rebuilt *c.* 1600, survives in fragments amid the present Hall Farm. The site of the earlier hall (medieval) is marked by a moated site, with fishponds, to the south of the church. The latter, apparently a 13th-century building, fell into ruin in the 17th century, when the greedy sheep had eaten up all the men (to use Sir Thomas

LEICESTER: castle gatehouse and north side of St Mary de Castro

64

More's phrase) but the Friends of Knaptoft hold a service here once a year in the summer.

Knighton (8) was a country village 50 years ago, but is now deeply embedded in Leicester. The church (St Mary Magdalene) was greatly enlarged (and improved) in 1960–2. Previously small and dark, it is now light and welcoming. It had been restored before in the 1860s and again in 1894, but the original late 13th-century tower remains, with an upper stage of the 15th century. A statue of St Mary Magdalene re-mains in a niche in the tower. The north aisle, originally the nave, retains its original roof.

Knighton Hall has a Queen Anne front, but the gabled back is early 17th century with an Elizabethan core. Throsby wrote in 1790 that it was then "an old low mansion, rather sequestered from view, but perhaps suitable to a gentleman on the decline of life". It is now the residence of the Vice-Chancellor of the University of Leicester.

Knipton (3) lies in the deep valley of the river Devon, in hilly wooded country quite unlike any other part of Leicestershire. Knipton Reservoir, just south-west of the village, was formed by damming the Devon. It is about 90 acres in extent and formerly served to supply the Nottingham and Grantham Canal (closed in 1929) with water. The wooded banks add greatly to the beauty of the landscape round here. Knipton is a neat "estate village" on the domain of the dukes of Rutland.

The church (All Saints) is of ironstone, mainly 13th century in date, except the rebuilt north aisle (1869). One of the rectors was the Rev.

LEICESTER: The Crescent, King Street

William Peters (1742–1818) described as "a happy pluralist"—he occupied many livings at once—and also as "a clever artist and pleasant colourist". He exhibited at the Royal Academy 1769–85, and was rector of Knipton 1788–1808. Many of his paintings were at Belvoir Castle and were destroyed in the great fire in 1816, but some survived, notably those of the 4th duke and his duchess. He greatly improved the rectory and its garden.

Knossington (6) village is clustered on high ground on the eastern boundary of Leicestershire, nearly 600 ft. above sea-level. It belonged to Owston Abbey, and passed at the Great Plunder (commonly known as the Dissolution) to Gregory, Lord Cromwell, son of Thomas Cromwell. The almshouses were founded in 1711 and rebuilt in 1821. The church (St Peter) was originally Decorated, but was over-restored in the 1880s. The font is Early English, and may be contemporary with the first mention of the church in 1199.

Laughton (8) is best reached by a beautiful drive through Gumley Park. The miniature Laughton Hills, rising to 560 ft., fall steeply and picturesquely to the banks of the Grand Union Canal, along which there is a quiet towpath walk from Theddingworth Lodge to Lubenham Lodge and thence (for the more energetic) to Foxton Locks.

The church (St Luke) is basically a 13th-century structure with a western bell-cote, all heavily restored or rebuilt in 1880, when the north and south aisles were destroyed. The nicest thing is a small slate memorial tablet to an old colonel—William Cole, who was also the squire—who served under King Charles I "of blessed memory" and three succeeding kings, for 58 years a commissioned officer. He died 27 March 1698 in his 85th year.

Launde (6) is now only a big H-shaped house in the rolling, wooded hill-country of east Leicestershire, on the site of an Augustinian priory founded in 1119 and dissolved in 1538. The name means "glade, pasture"—hence our modern word "lawn". Of the priory, the chancel alone remains. The site was acquired at the Dissolution by Thomas Cromwell, Henry VIII's great minister of state, and his son Gregory built a manor house where the priory had stood. A little remains of this date; much else is late 17th century, and much is restored. Gregory, later Lord Cromwell, died here in 1551. His tomb is in the chapel of the house: of it Pevsner says it is "one of the purest monuments of the Early Renaissance in England, very grand and restrained".

Leicester (5) is at first sight a totally uninteresting Midland city. Harold Nicolson, who represented the western side of it in Parliament for many years, records in the late summer of 1954: "We passed through Leicester, and I gazed out on that ugly and featureless city, thinking how strange it was that I had for so long been identified with those brick houses with their ironwork railings and their clean little steps." It is indeed a desert of hundreds of acres of little red-brick terrace houses put up in the last three decades of the 19th century, and hundreds of acres more of housing estates of the 1930s, and after that the modern sprawl for miles round all the edges except the south-east. The quickest and pleasantest way out of modern Leicester is down the Stoughton Road in the suburb of Stoneygate (formerly the Roman road to Godmanchester) running south-eastwards into green pastures within two or three minutes from leaving the seething London Road.

The city proper contains rather under 300,000 people, but the conurbating flow has swamped over villages in all directions but one, and is estimated to house just about half a million people. As the total population of the geographical county is considerably under three-quarters of a million (723,000 to be precise, in 1967) this means that two people out of three live inside this amorphous mass. Yet the strange fact is that Leicester, or the little bit of it in the old heart, is one of the historic cities of England, and still retains a good deal of interest to the intelligent traveller, from the Roman to the mid-20th century.

Since the street plan of the city is bewildering to the visitor, though it has its own logic when interpreted historically, and since the one-way traffic system is baffling to all except those inured to it daily, it is best to forget the car. Not that one can ever see anything worth seeing from a car anyway. And since in my opinion a planned itinerary in a busy city is nearly impossible, I have written about the things worth seeing by dividing them into "periods"—unsatisfactory as any scheme like this is bound to be—in the hope that those who seek only the Roman, or the medieval, or the Victorian, or the Modern, will find their way to it without toiling through masses of things that do not appeal to them. "Periods" overlap also, in so many interesting buildings, but I have coped with this difficulty the best way I can.

I have also dealt with the places that Leicester has swallowed up in recent years (e.g. Belgrave, Knighton, Evington, and many others) under their own alphabetical headings, in order to make the whole vast area more manageable. Finally, in this general guidance to the reader, there is a first-class guide to the city by Professor Jack Simmons, obtainable from the City Information Office in Bishop Street, at a modest price, which gives more detail about the places of interest than I can give here.

Two features of the Leicester scene which do not fall into any one period, however, deserve special mention. The first is the great open-air market, typical of so many in the Midlands and the North of England. This has been held on the same site since at least the 13th century and almost certainly from long before that. Though there is some market every weekday, the best days to browse around it are Wednesday, Friday, and Saturday. It is a sight not to be missed by anyone who visits the city.

The second feature is quite different: it is the New Walk, which runs parallel to the London Road for nearly a mile, tree-lined and car-free all the way except where one has to cope briefly with a cross-road.

Engraved slate in
Leicester cathedral

First laid out in 1785, Pevsner says it is unique in England. As he says, too, the buildings are nothing special and some are bad. In places the Walk has been allowed to crumble with "planning blight" but no doubt this will be put right. Architecturally, it is a pleasant exercise in domestic building from the early 19th century near the bottom to the favourite Jacobean of the well-to-do of the 1890s at the top near the Victoria Park Gates.

Now, period by period as far as possible, here are the major things worth seeing in the city proper:

Roman: Leicester was founded just before the Roman conquest, and at the conquest became the capital of the Coritani; hence it was called *Ratae Coritanorum*. The finest remains of this period are in St Nicholas Street. These are the *Jewry Wall*, part of the front wall of the town hall or basilica, *c.* A.D. 130, and the excavated site of the forum, later the public baths, of the same date. Much of the material from this site can be seen in the *Jewry Wall Museum*, one of the several admirable Leicester museums, which specialises in the archaeology of the city and the region.

   Of the same period are two tesselated pavements which belonged to important buildings, one beneath the former Great Central railway station, the other under no. 50 St Nicholas Street. Enquiries about these should be made at the Jewry Wall Museum.

Saxon: *St Nicholas church*, close beside the Jewry Wall, is one of the best-known Anglo-Saxon churches of England. Some experts think it may be as early as the 7th century, others put it at 9th–10th century. Also Norman and later work.

Norman and Medieval: several major monuments in the older part of the town. Behind the 1690s façade of the *Castle* is the original hall of the Norman castle, *c.* 1150. Much medieval building also. *St Mary de Castro* church, as the name says,

LEICESTER cathedral

was the castle church, begun about 1107, with much fine early Norman work. The stone sedilia of *c.* 1180 are the finest of their kind in England. The church has a complicated building history (*see* Simmons, *Guide*). Good array of "civic" monuments over the centuries.

Of the other churches in the old town, *All Saints* (Highcross Street) dates mostly from *c.* 1300, chancel of 1829, Norman west doorway, and much other detail, all worth seeing; and *St Margaret's*, a rather grand parish church on an ancient site, now mostly a late 15th-century building. Note the monument of Bishop Penny, 1520, who was abbot of Leicester 1496–1504 and then bishop of Bangor and later of Carlisle.

The *Guildhall* in Guildhall Lane is one of the most remarkable civic buildings in England. Again a somewhat complicated building history, beginning as early as about 1390 (the Great Hall). Fine Carolean Mayor's Parlour. Town library housed here. The whole forms a beautiful courtyard, medieval and later in date and atmosphere.

Surrounding the original castle was a large bailey, the "new work" of the 15th century, called the *Newarke* today. Two fine gateways of that date survive. Like the Guildhall, which narrowly escaped destruction when the new Town Hall was built in the 1870s, these gateways have had their anxious times. On the whole, though, the City of Leicester has a far better record in preserving its important ancient buildings than most towns. This may not be saying much by English standards, but the fact remains that the Leicester city council has usually risen to the occasion when public spirit called for it.

Tudor and Later: a very varied lot of interesting buildings survive. In the Newarke is the *Chantry House* (1511) and next to it the 16th–17th century building known today as the *Newarke Houses Museum*. The two buildings together form another of the first-class Leicester museums, this one being devoted to local bygones—costume, etc.

In Highcross Street is the original Elizabethan *Grammar School*, built in 1573, now and for long used as a warehouse. This is a major blot on the city's reputation, that it has never felt impelled to rescue the school in which so many generations of Leicester boys received a good education and went on to govern their town. It would make a splendid museum of a specialist kind.

In Churchgate, on the way to St Margaret's church, is the principal Nonconformist chapel, the *Great Meeting* (1708), the main structure unaltered. Leicester has always been a Nonconformist stronghold; this tradition is still strong and shows itself in several ways to the discerning eye. Good Swithland slate headstones in the burial ground.

In Friar Lane, New Street, and St Martin's, may be seen a nice lot of good Georgian town houses, now mostly offices. The *County Rooms* in Hotel Street were built by a Leicester architect (John

LEICESTER : The White House, by Ernest Gimson

70

LEICESTER University: The Engineering Building by Stirling & Gowan

Johnson) and opened in 1800. Fine façade, and a grand ballroom inside on the first floor.

Nineteenth Century: Leicester was still a relatively small town in 1800 (about 17,000 people) and grew enormously during the next three generations. Hence, despite the number of earlier "monuments", it strikes the casual visitor as a rather dull Victorian town. In fact, much of the 19th century, too, is worthy of close study. Among the larger buildings on a civic scale are the *Museum and Art Gallery* (1849) in the New Walk, built by J. A. Hansom, who gave his name to the hansom cab. He also built the curious "Pork-Pie Chapel" for the Baptists in Belvoir Street in 1845. The *Corn Exchange* in the Market Place is an attractive building of 1851 by Ordish, another local architect, its graceful proportions rather hidden by the busy market below.

Somewhat earlier than these buildings is *St George's church*, behind the Police Station in Charles Street, built in 1823–5 by William Parsons, gutted by fire in 1911 and rebuilt at once by W. D.

Caroë. It was the first church to be built in Leicester since the Reformation, and retains the stately proportions of early Victorian Gothic, with lofty arcades. The churchyard, too, is an oasis among the dreary brick factories and offices of this part of the town.

Holy Trinity was built by S. Smirke in 1838, and tremendously recast by S. S. Teulon later in century.

Among the more purely Victorian buildings is the *Clock Tower* of 1868—small and slightly silly now among the seething modern traffic, but affectionately regarded by older generations at least as the true centre of the town. Exiles from Leicester always used to ask "How's the old Clock Tower?" when visited far from home. Does anybody ask it now? The *Town Hall* in Town Hall Square is a very successful piece of Victorian Renaissance work of 1874–6, well worth contemplating; and in Granby Street the National Provincial Bank and the Midland Bank form a good contrast between two different decades and styles of Victorian, the former

chaste and still classical, the latter polychromatic and exuberantly Gothic. A great deal of Leicester amply rewards the Victorian enthusiast, not least the tree-lined suburb of Stoneygate on the south side of the town (reached along the London Road) where one may study the housing of the wealthy over half a century of opulent domestic building.

St Leonard 1866–7, and St Paul, 1870–1, are by Ordish and Traylen. St Peter is by G. E. Street, 1873–4.

Lastly, the cathedral church of St Martin: though on a very ancient site, the present church (a cathedral only since 1926) was so often and vigorously restored during the 19th century that it is best accepted as such. The noble tower and spire, recognisable from afar, are entirely of 1862–7 by Brandon. The monuments and fittings of the church are well worthy of study. As Jack Simmons says, "they are a memorial to the civic, social, and military life of Leicester during the past four hundred years", and those who treasure English provincial life, as

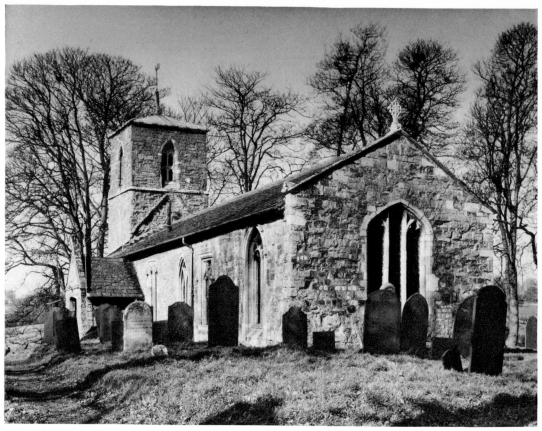

LITTLE STRETTON: the church before the unfortunate removal of the gravestones in 1969

I do, will find an amble round St Martin's very satisfying.

Modern: here one is swayed by prejudices and lack of perspective. Bodley's church of *All Souls* in Aylestone Road (1907) is cool and elegant inside, with glass by Comper. The *De Montfort Hall* on the edge of Victoria Park was built in 1912 as a temporary affair, and has remained as the best concert hall the city possesses, and a decent building as well. Near by is Lutyens' fine *War Memorial* to the dead of Leicester in two German Wars.

The largest group of modern buildings is to be found on the *University* site. Of these, the Engineering Building excited great controversy when it was built a few years ago. Some regard it as a major achievement, others as aggressive and gimmicky. Go and judge for yourself. The other buildings of the University strike me as commonplace, and occasionally worse than that. But no names, no pack-drill. To me the best part of the University building is the old front of 1836–7, when it was built as a lunatic asylum, still in the classical tradition. Other recent buildings obtrude themselves upon the view in all directions in the city, and the earnest seeker after them need only take his bearings as he goes along. Old-fashioned and no doubt purblind, I can see little to enjoy in them, but this will all sort itself out in the end.

At any rate, Leicester, which makes so unfavourable a first impression, deserves a couple of days' exploration on foot. Gastronomically though, an important element in strenuous exploration in a busy town, I have found it quite depressing. It has its moments, but they are sadly few. Perhaps it is an odd hangover of the Nonconformist tradition of the town that one cannot discuss food and drink seriously without being regarded as a bibulous glutton. Also, there is too much money in the Midlands, and a large bill is too readily regarded as evidence of quality. Alas for the poor among us!

Leire (7) is a mysterious place-name. The experts say "very likely an old river-name", probably *Legra* and identical with Loire in France which had the name of *Ligeris* in ancient Gaul. The village is rather dull and so is the church (St Peter), which was rebuilt, except the Perpendicular tower, in 1867–8.

Lindley (7) lies just off the A.5 (the Roman Watling Street). It is no longer a village, having been wiped out by the squire John Hardwick in the year 1500. He has a place in history because he met the Earl of Richmond (later Henry VII) at Atherstone, a few miles away, and led him with his army to Bosworth Field "whereby the earl got the advantage of ground, wind, and sun" and won a decisive victory on 22 August 1485. The earl's army marched along the Roman road through Fenny Drayton to its eve-of-battle encampment on White Moors, just south of Shenton village.

Lindley Hall (demolished in 1926) was also notable as the birthplace of William Burton the antiquary (born 1575), author of *The Description of Leicestershire* (1622) and of his younger brother Robert Burton, born here 1577 and celebrated author of *The Anatomy of Melancholy* (1621).

Little Bowden (9), now in the suburbs of Market Harborough, has an attractive ironstone rectory dated 1627, with the initials AM : RM. The church (St Nicholas) is long and low, neat and decent. No tower, but a west bell-cote so common among the smaller churches of the East Midlands. Mostly an early 14th-century building (see especially the north aisle and arcade) with a 15th-century clerestory. The nave is probably 13th century; chancel mostly rebuilt in the 19th century by Bodley.

Little Dalby (6), a small village with a heavy Victorian church hidden on a wooded hill, but well worth a solemn pilgrimage. Let us begin with the hall, once the home of the Hartopps, and now divided into flats. The original house was built by William Hartopp who was buying land here in the 1580s. The west wing was added in 1682, the east wing 1816: the centre was rebuilt from 1838 onwards. Here the Hartopps (later Burns-Hartopp) lived in style until 1950. At the height of their opulence—Eton and Christ Church, the Oxford and Cambridge, Travellers, and Carlton clubs—they owned more than 34,000 acres (mostly in Ireland). The hall is chiefly famous for the fact that the housekeeper to the Hartopps in the reign of Queen Anne, one Mrs Orton, perfected

Stilton cheese here: but Stilton has a longer history than this (see the Introduction), and it only became widely known when it was made at Dalby.

The church (St James) was rebuilt regardless of expense, as well it might be, by the architect Brandon in 1851–3: ponderous, especially the west tower and spire, almost suburban, with stained glass by Pugin and Kempe. Despite their centuries of great wealth, the Hartopps have left no monuments at all, only a few nearly illegible slabs and brass tablets at the west end. Still, it is redolent of the opulent Victorian age: Hartopp squires and parsons. The Rev. Samuel Hartopp was 63 years rector of Cold Overton and Little Dalby (1789 to 1852), and his kinsman Edward Bourchier Hartopp was squire for 71 years, having succeeded to his huge estates in 1813 at the age of four. In this heavy church, so unlikeable at first sight, one catches the faint echoes of this monumental age. Thank God it is only an echo now, despite the pathos one cannot help feeling as an historian for a vanished age and eyelids closed in "morningless and unawakening sleep".

Little Stretton (8) lies just off the Roman (Gartree) road from Leicester to Godmanchester. Attractive collection of 18th-century farmhouses and cottages with a red-brick Georgian manor house. The church (St John the Baptist) is very appealing. Essentially a Norman nave, with a chancel rebuilt about 1300. The tower, with a low pyramidal roof, was added in the late 13th century, the upper stage rebuilt later. Font of about 1300, some old bench-ends, altar-rails of early 17th century, and a pulpit of 1776. All around is deep, quiet Leicestershire at its best, with the incomparable King's Norton church not far away, and Galby too: a nice afternoon's outing from the urban noise and rush of Leicester.

Littlethorpe (8), near Narborough, has a very good 16th-century farmhouse, built by a rising Leicestershire yeoman, John Bent, about 1560. Otherwise not an interesting village except for a few late Georgian red-brick houses.

pp 74–75 The Royal Arms at LOCKINGTON (1704) and at neighbouring KEGWORTH (1684)

Lockington (1) has a spacious village church (St Nicholas), mainly 13th century but so enlarged in the early 14th that it has that air about it. Externally not remarkable, but inside completely unrestored in fabric and furnishings, the latter being especially interesting. Fine wooden tympanum of 1704 above the chancel screen, "a remarkable piece of work of unusual design and excellent detail . . . much superior in execution to any of the few examples of its kind which still remain in England" (Hamilton Thompson). Good pulpit and reading-desk, 18th century also. Gallery of the same date. But the box-pews were unfortunately removed in 1953. Some complete 15th-century benches survive; altar-rails of Laudian period (*c.* 1630).

Much work was done to the church in the 15th century: the tower was then added, and internally the chancel and parclose screens erected. The nave and aisle roofs belong to this time of modernisation, when the clerestory was added to the nave. Brick floors throughout, some medieval glass in the windows, several mural monuments and medieval floor slabs. With all this, the interest of this church is not exhausted: one could wander round it again and again. The Bainbrigges were squires here in the 17th and 18th centuries, and built the present hall (late 17th century, but stone-faced about 1800).

Loddington (6) lies in a remote countryside, more like Devon than Leicestershire: hilly, winding lanes, and wooded. The church (St Michael) stands alone. Ironstone, as usual in these parts, with a large square west tower. The south doorway is Norman but basically it is a 14th-century interior (see the north and south arcades), with a Perpendicular chancel and clerestory. Screen erected 1859. Pulpit 17th century; some old glass in south-east window of the chancel. The churchyard contains many nice examples of carved Ketton headstones—we are very near Rutland here—redolent of the 18th century and the early 19th.

The hall is described in the *Direct-*

ory of 1846 as "a large and handsome modern mansion". In Conduit Close, about one mile north-east of the hall, are the remains of a building covering two wells of clear, pure water, formerly carried by lead pipes to Launde Priory. All round here is lovely withdrawn country—leading to Launde, Withcote, Robin-a-Tiptoe Hill, Owston and its ancient monastic woods and ruined abbey, and so on through a long summer afternoon and evening.

Long Clawson (2) is a large village of remarkably irregular plan in the Vale of Belvoir. There are fine views of the wooded escarpment to the south, and equally fine views into Nottinghamshire from the top of Clawson Hill. Many decent brick farmhouses and cottages of the standard Leicestershire type. Manor house south of the church built about 1600.

The church has the very unusual dedication to St Remigius, a great apostle of the French who ruled over the see of Rheims in the late 5th–early 6th century and baptised the Frankish king Clovis there in the year 496. The present church is a large cruciform building with a good Decorated central tower. Most of the church is early 14th century in date but the *Little Guide* says that the transepts were destroyed in the 17th century and rebuilt in the closing years of the 19th century. A 12th-century window built into the south transept may be all that is left of the Norman church.

Long Whatton (4) is a village that goes on and on—as its name implies —along the Loughborough–Melbourne road. Interesting for its vernacular building. Framework-knitting was carried on here into the 20th century.

The church (All Saints) has a Norman tower at the end of the south aisle—a most unusual position. The font is also Norman, but the rest of the church is Decorated, though greatly restored in the 1860s. Elizabethan pulpit brought from Colston Basset in Nottinghamshire. Good Perpendicular screen. Whatton Hall is 1802, restored 1876 after a fire.

Loughborough (4, 5) is the largest town in Leicestershire, after Leicester itself. Despite its grimy red-brick appearance, so redolent of the industrial East Midlands at their dreariest, it is a market town of considerable antiquity. It lies astride the A.6—the main road from London to Leicester and Manchester—which does not add to its gaiety. The market (on Thursdays) is a good example of an open-air Midland market certainly established by the year 1221, and even then perhaps an old institution. The November Fair dates from 1228. It is now held on the second Thursday in November.

The new University of Technology has some excellent modern buildings, more striking and pleasing (in my view) than those of the somewhat older University of Leicester which rarely rises above the commonplace. The town as a whole is dreary, but the outskirts on the Charnwood Forest side are pleasantly suburban.

The church (All Saints) is fine and spacious, mainly 14th and 15th century in date, much restored by Gilbert Scott in 1860–3. The tower, good Perpendicular, would do credit to Somerset. The nave is flanked by early 14th-century arcades. Contemporary windows in the aisles (*c.*1300). Fine 15th-century clerestory with contemporary nave roof. Chancel rebuilt in late 15th century.

Other notable buildings are the Town Hall (1855) in the Market Place, the Baptist Chapel (1828) in Baxtergate, and Hastings House, an early classical work (1838) by Gilbert Scott. Holy Trinity church in Moor Lane is by Blomfield. The Carillon Tower (1922–3) is a notable element in the Loughborough scene. Loughborough is the home of a famous firm of bell-founders (Taylors) who came here from Oxford in 1859.

Lowesby (5) lies about 500 ft. up in the east Leicestershire hills. Only the church and hall remain. The village was finally depopulated by the Ashbys in 1487 and enclosed for cattle and sheep pastures. The site of the "lost village" lies immediately east of the park boundary and west of the road to Cold Newton, i.e. between the Cold Newton road and the park. It is clearly marked by house-sites and fish-ponds.

Lowesby Hall is a handsome brick mansion, probably dating from the last years of the 17th century. The gardens were laid out by Lutyens about 1912. The church (All Saints) shows traces of the 13th century, but basically it is 14th century with Perpendicular additions (e.g. the north and south arcades, clerestory, and top stage of the tower). Lit by oil-lamps. Monument to Richard Woollaston, 1689. The public road runs through a small and attractive park. There was a notable pottery at Lowesby in the 1840s and 1850s. White says (1846) that the pottery was "highly celebrated for its garden and chimney pots. Bricks and tiles are also extensively manufactured here, and there have been made here of the 'Lowesby Terra Cotta' many beautifully enamelled and painted *Vases* etc. after the antique." This manufacture seems to have ceased by 1864, when only a brick and tile maker remained, but some nice examples of the Lowesby vases, etc., may be seen in the Newarke Museum at Leicester.

Lubenham (8) has a most attractive church (All Saints), externally of varied levels and colours like a Cotman drawing: ironstone and limestone as usual, with Colly Weston slated roof. Inside a delightful country interior—box-pews, three-decker pulpit, a few medieval bench-ends. Whitewashed walls and clear glass give it an 18th-century air. Mixed medieval periods in the structure, the oldest bit being a pier in the north arcade of about 1190–1200. Mostly though it is a 13th-century church, early and late. But the placid Georgian country interior is the thing here.

Lutterworth (7) is a small country town which has seen better days, judging by what remains of handsome houses of an earlier age. Note the town hall of 1836, Workhouse of 1840, and a Congregational chapel of 1777. But there is much other decent or even notable building. The church (St Mary) is typical Leicestershire in date, i.e. late 13th-century to early 14th. Good aisle roofs. The top stage of the tower is early 18th-century Gothic. Pulpit of

MARKET HARBOROUGH: The Swan inn sign

15th century (so it cannot be Wycliffe's, who was rector here in the late 14th century). He died here on 30 December 1384 (monument by Westmacott, 1837). His bones were dug up and burnt in 1428 and the ashes thrown into the little River Swift at the bottom end of the town. Some good Swithland slate headstones in the churchyard.

Market Bosworth (4) "is a small ancient market town, seated on a pleasant eminence", says the directory of 1846. It is a name famous in English history for the battle fought some two miles to the south on 22 August 1485—a classic piece of English soil, second only to Hastings

in the annals of battle (*see* the Introduction). Yet the site is not marked in any way, except by a small stone structure over the spring where Richard drank in the heat of the fight, shown as *Well* on the Ordnance map.

The little town is centred upon the market place and has been for nearly 700 years, for the Wednesday market was granted in 1285. There is a good deal of vernacular and better building, including the grammar school in 1828 Tudor, and the classical workhouse of 1836.

The church (St Peter) stands between Bosworth Park and the town, with a fine tower and spire visible from afar. Most of it is early 14th

century, somewhat remodelled in the 15th century. Thus the south aisle, clerestory, and chancel are Perpendicular, when the piers of the arcades were also refashioned. Some glass by Kempe and a monument to the Rev. John Dixie (1719). The Dixies bought the manor in 1567 and are still there, but no longer at the hall, which is now a hospital. The hall is a rather grand Queen Anne house, but as Pevsner says "much interfered with in 1888" and later.

Market Harborough (8, 9) is a lively market town, too lively at times, for the A.6 cuts through the middle of it and spoils a fine bit of townscape, with the magnificent tower and spire

78

of the parish church dominating the market place and the little grammar school of 1614. The town grew up in Henry II's time at the crossing place over the Welland, now a poor little stream, and halfway between the two important medieval towns of Northampton and Leicester. It acquired a weekly market in 1203. The High Street is bright, and retains much good building up and down its length, notably no. 29, and the two big inns —the Angel and the Three Swans. Town Hall of 1788.

The church of St Dionysius rises straight out of the market place, with no burial ground as it was in origin a daughter-church to Great Bowden and had no right to bury. This adds enormously to the visual effect, the tower and broach spire being one of the grandest in all England. The church was begun in the time of Bishop Grosseteste of Lincoln (1235–54) and was given its unusual dedication as St Dionysius was the special study of the learned bishop. Nothing seems to remain of this early church. The tower and spire date from 1300 onwards, built of ashlar limestone; the rest of the church, built of ironstone, does not begin to compare in grandeur with these. The body of the church underwent the usual changes in the Perpendicular period (cf. the arcades and the original aisle roofs). But the north and south galleries, with box-pews, of 1836 really give the feeling to the interior. A good town church, but poor in furnishings. The ruined church of St Mary in Arden is a sad thing but interesting. It was rebuilt in 1693–9 by Richard Dormer. A good town for pottering round the shops, some of them still agreeably old-fashioned.

Markfield (4) is a large village on the southern edge of Charnwood Forest. The older houses are built of the rough forest stone; the village was formerly noted for the number of its poor framework-knitters. The church (St Michael) was much altered in the late 1820s and underwent a further drastic "restoration and enlargement" in 1865, when the chancel was rebuilt.

Measham (1) is an unlovely colliery village on the main Ashby–Tam-

worth road. The church (St Laurence) is mostly early 14th century with the usual Perpendicular porch and clerestory added, but the tower was rebuilt in the 1730s. Measham Hall, $1\frac{1}{4}$ miles east of the village, is a good mid-Georgian house, off the road to Swepstone.

Medbourne (9) is a large village with a long history. It is almost certain that it has been continuously occupied since Roman times. A large Roman villa was discovered here in 1721, and many other Roman and Saxon remains have since been found on the site. The Roman Gartree Road runs close to the village, on its way to cross the Welland and heading towards Godmanchester in Huntingdonshire. White's *Directory* of 1846 records that in a field just north-west of the village were the remains of "entrenchments" covering an area of about a mile square. "Tradition says that in this field once stood a city called *Medenborough*, which was destroyed by fire." This is nonsense as it stands, but there must be some archaeological explanation for such a large area, with evident traces of former buildings.

Medbourne has always been a prosperous village, and it still contains a considerable number of interesting houses, large and small. The T-shaped Manor House at the eastern end of the village is, behind its 17th-century façade, a remarkable survival of a late 13th-century house. The Old Hall, south-east of the church, is an H-plan house of 17th-century date, built soon after 1650. The whole village is worth exploring on foot. Near the church is a medieval bridge of three arches, with a modern handrail. The village was granted a weekly market and an annual fair in 1266.

The church (St Giles) has an odd plan, and has been much altered, so that its architectural history is obscure. An earlier church was probably destroyed by fire about 1250, and another cruciform church, on an elaborate plan, was begun before 1300. But the original plan was apparently abandoned, and what is left is chiefly interesting for

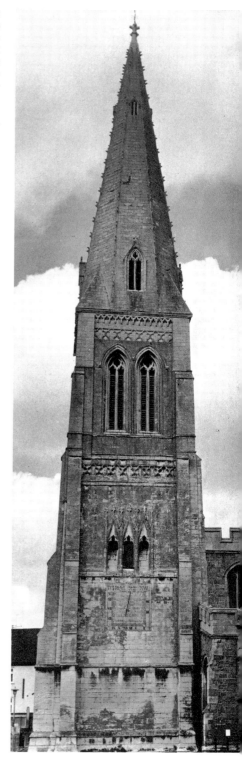

MARKET HARBOROUGH

79

its south aisle and south transept. There is no north aisle, and a north transept, begun about 1300, is now represented by a modern one. The chancel was rebuilt in 1876.

The village kept its open fields until as late as 1844, in a high state of cultivation. Throsby has an interesting description of their excellent farming in 1790. The old open-field system has been much maligned by historians, most of them too much influenced by the propagandist Arthur Young.

Melton Mowbray (6) is a pleasant market town of about 18,000 people on the River Wreak, which is called the Eye above the town. The former name is Scandinavian, the latter Old English, and it indicates that Melton must have been a kind of border town between the English and the Scandinavian parts of the Danelaw. It takes its second name from the great Norman family of Mowbray who were holding the manor by 1125. The *Little Guide* (1924 edition) calls it "the hunting metropolis which in the summer is a quiet country town, in the winter one of the brightest and busiest resorts in England". Hunting has declined enormously since 1939 so far as Melton is concerned: indeed what is to be seen today is of purely historic interest.

One of the most interesting features of the town is the open-air market, characteristic of so many Midland towns. It takes up several streets in the town on Tuesdays and on Saturdays, in addition to the covered market. The Tuesday market is perhaps the better one and is well worth while attending, especially the market just before Christmas, which one would go a long way to see if it were in another country. It is an extremely ancient institution, being recorded as a profitable concern as early as 1077, and certainly dates from Saxon times. It has probably been held on a Tuesday for the last thousand years. Back in the mid-19th century Melton also had five annual fairs.

The Old English settled here as early as the 5th or 6th century; one of their pagan cemeteries has been found on the outskirts of the town. Later it became an important Anglo-Danish settlement and the mother-parish of a large area of land—its first name means "middle *tun*". The parish church (St Mary) existed before the Norman conquest, though nothing remains from this early date. As Pevsner says, it is "the stateliest and most impressive of all churches in Leicestershire", and when the diocese of Leicester was revived in 1926 it was seriously considered as the possible cathedral for the new diocese. It is a superb cruciform church with north and south transepts which themselves are aisled, giving at first sight a complicated plan to the interior. Only three other churches in England have this elaborate plan—St Mary Redcliffe at Bristol, Patrington in the East Riding of Yorkshire, and Faversham in Kent. The first impression from the outside is of a late Perpendicular church with a particularly magnificent clerestory and tower, the latter spoilt from some angles by an inferior turret stair. The lower part of the tower is, however, early 13th century in date. The interior is mainly between 1280–1330, the great period for Leicestershire church-building. Notice especially the west porch with its highly decorated work of about 1330. The church was completed by the building of a north vestry in 1532. There are fewer monuments than one might expect in such a grand building. In the south aisle is the effigy of a cross-legged knight, identified as "Lord Hamon Beler, brother to the Lord Mowbray", and in the south transept is an alabaster effigy of a lady of the late 14th century.

On the whole the town looks bright and cheerful, with many decent 18th-century and early 19th-century houses. The most notable buildings are the so-called Anne of Cleves House, near the church, which is basically 15th century in date and was either a chantry house belonging to the church or perhaps the dwelling-house of one of the rich wool merchants who must have subscribed heavily to the magnificent enlargement of the church in the late 15th century. Opposite the church is the so-called Maison Dieu founded as an almshouse by Robert Hudson in 1640. In the Market Place the former Swan Inn retains a fine porch over the pavement. The Roman Catholic church of St John, in Thorpe Road, is by Pugin, 1842. St Mary's Hospital was formerly the workhouse, built in 1836. The elegant bridge over the canal and river, by which one enters the town from Leicester, was constructed in 1832.

Melton became the hunting metropolis of England early in the 19th century and was frequented by the nobility and gentry from all parts of the country during the hunting season. As late as 1939 it was said that, at the beginning of the hunting season, a thousand fine hunters were stabled in the town and the stables, now frequently converted into flats or put to other uses, can still be seen by those who take an interest in this kind of social history.

A number of the large houses at which the richest established themselves for the season are still to be seen.

Craven Lodge on Burton Hill was almost entirely rebuilt by the Hon. W. Craven, who purchased the property in 1856. The 4th Marquess of Hastings (Mad Harry) purchased the property only a few months before his miserable death. The lodge is noted for its association with the royal family. In the spring of 1923 the Prince of Wales became a member of the Craven Lodge Club and during the following summer an annexe was built for the privacy and comfort of the Prince. Later it became the hunting quarters of the then Duke of York, the Duke of Gloucester, and of Prince George. It is now a residential special school.

Wyndham Lodge is now the Memorial Hospital on Ankle Hill. This stone-built house was erected in 1867 by Mr W. A. Chaplain on or near the site of the Old Wyndham Lodge, the home of the Waterloo veteran, Colonel Wyndham, who left Melton in 1852 to become the Governor of the Tower of London. In 1922 this Lodge was opened as a hospital.

Warwick Lodge, at the top of Ankle Hill, was formerly called Hamilton Lodge and was built by Gavin Lord Hamilton in 1902: later purchased by Frances Countess of Warwick, one of the numerous mistresses of King

F

Edward VII. This is now the Rural District Council Offices.

Egerton Lodge, in Wilton Road, was built in 1829 by Thomas Earl of Wilton. He married the daughter and sole heiress of Thomas Egerton and took her surname, hence the name of Egerton Lodge. Lord Wilton greatly altered and expanded the property, employing Wyatt as his architect, and Egerton Lodge became the very heart of the hunting metropolis. The Duke of Wellington, Viscount and Viscountess Beaconsfield, and Edward Prince of Wales were all visitors here. The Duke and Duchess of Cambridge and their daughter Princess Mary Adelaide of Teck were frequent visitors also.

The Lodge, hidden away at the bottom of a drive off Dalby Road, was the home of Sir Francis Grant, the President of the Royal Academy, who lived here for forty years. One of his best-known paintings is "The Melton Breakfast". In the 1870s Edward Prince of Wales was entertained here, and in 1878 the famous explorer, H. M. Stanley, came here to rest and recuperate after his strenuous journeys in Africa, his host being James Gordon Bennett, proprietor of the *New York Herald*, who had financed the expedition.

Coventry House is at the bottom of Burton End, facing the railway. It is probably the oldest of Melton's hunting boxes, but its early history is obscure. At the close of the 18th century there were two houses, one of which was called Claret Lodge and, according to the renowned Dick Christian, it was rightly so called. Among those who have resided here are the Duke and Duchess of Cleveland and the Marquis of Worcester. The eccentric Marquis of Waterford also lived here who, in one night in the spring of 1837 with the help of some of his friends, actually did "paint the town red". In the 1850s the Hon. H. A. Coventry purchased the house and enlarged it. In 1877 King Edward VII, as Prince of Wales, stayed here for several days. Soon afterwards Count Zborowski became the owner. This Polish millionaire was killed in a motor-car race at Nice in April 1909 and is buried in Burton Lazars churchyard.

Brudenell House is in Burton End, next to the Boat Inn. It was here that

Nottingham Street, MELTON MOWBRAY

MELTON MOWBRAY: the derelict North Station

the well-known Viscount Brudenell lived before he went to the Crimea to gain immortal fame in the Charge of the Light Brigade. After this exploit he returned to his Melton home as Earl of Cardigan, and it remained his winter home until his death in 1868.

A little farther up Burton Street is *The Manor House*, now occupied by the East Midlands Electricity Board. When the old manor house was demolished in the 1870s, Lord Melbourne built a new house on the site. In 1873 the then owner was host to Edward Prince of Wales for several days. Edward appears to have slept in more beds than Queen Elizabeth. *Sysonby Lodge*, in Nottingham Road, is now the offices of Stewarts & Lloyds. For many years it was known as Plymouth Lodge after the 6th Earl of Plymouth who rebuilt it in the early 19th century. Among those who have hunted from here were Lord Beatty, Sir Winston Churchill, and the American Vanderbilts. *Staveley Lodge* in Nottingham Road

is now part of Production Engineering Research Assoc. It was built in the 1860s by Thomas Hickson, who named the house after his maternal grandfather, Christopher Staveley. Among the distinguished visitors to this lodge was the Earl of Oxford and Asquith. The lodge came into the possession of Her Highness the Maharanee of Cooch Behar who, at immense expense, transformed the place into something resembling an Indian Palace.

After all this aristocratic nonsense, it is a pleasure to turn to *Elgin Lodge*, in Scalford Road, by the entrance to the approach to the old Great Northern Railway Station. This house was built in 1814 by John Ferneley (1782–1860) and he lived here until his death. He painted most of his famous pictures here and even in his lifetime could command a fee of 2,000 guineas for a picture. In the *Directory* of 1846 he is listed among the three "artists" living at Melton in that time. A tablet in the chancel of Melton Mowbray church calls him "animal painter of Melton Mow-

bray, died 3 June 1860 aged 78 years". In 1877 George Whyte Melville, the sporting novelist, lived here.

There are numerous smaller hunting boxes scattered about Melton which the untiring pilgrim will no doubt find for himself.

It only remains to say about Melton that it has a supreme distinction of producing two gastronomic specialities of national fame—pork pies and Stilton cheese. The real Stilton cheese is only made in Melton and in a few villages round about, and a lawsuit was fought recently to establish this monopoly of the name. As for the pork pies, they have been made here since at least the 1830s, and though there are possible rivals in Leicester and elsewhere, those of Melton Mowbray would take a great deal of beating.

Misterton (8) is now little more than a church and a hall, but was once a considerable village along the old road which runs through the park, the modern road representing a later

83

diversion. The church (St Leonard) is mainly a 14th-century building, with good Decorated window tracery. But the site is an ancient one, as the name means "minster"-tun, i.e. the site of an early *monasterium* or mother-church for a large area around. There are some good bench-ends of Henry VIII's time, and monuments to the Poulteneys (Sir Michael, 1567, and John, 1637). They derived from the now "lost village" of Poultney, 1½ miles north-east of Misterton, the site being represented by Great Poultney Farm, close to the infant river Swift. The township was probably deserted and converted to cattle and sheep pastures before 1500,

and the Poulteneys took up their residence at the hall in Misterton, which is described in the 1846 *Directory* as "an ancient mansion". In the small park were some lofty trees which were said to have been standing in the time of Richard III, but on what authority I do not know. The Poulteneys died out at Misterton in 1672.

Sir John de Poultney (d. 1349) was one of this family, a notable Lord Mayor of London in the 1330s, who became wealthy enough to advance money to King Edward III. The city parish of St Lawrence Pountney takes its second name from him. Another descendant of this old Leicestershire

family was Sir William Pulteney, Earl of Bath (1684–1764) the states-man after whom the Pulteney Bridge at Bath is named.

Mountsorrel (5), strung out along the thunderous A.6, is much more interesting than would appear from a harassed passage in a car. It is first recorded in 1152 as *Munt Sorel*, when it had a strong Norman castle on the granite hill behind the village guarding a sort of pass between this crag and the river Soar, the A.6 being even then a major road between important towns. It may by analogy be named after Mont-Sorel near Rennes in Brittany, or Montsoreau near Saumur. Nothing remains of the castle today. The castle hill has been extensively quarried for the highly durable red granite or syenite which was much used for street paving and the waste for road sur-facing. It was also used for mill-stones and kerbstones, and later (when ways were found of fashioning it) for churches and secular buildings round about. The quarries are still worked commercially in a big way.

Mountsorrel was elevated to a market town as early as 1292, and given an eight-day fair which was famous for centuries, so much so that Mountsorrel families who emigrated to the United States in the 19th century continued to celebrate it far from home.

Despite much destruction in recent years, the town retains a great deal of highly interesting vernacular building and is well worth exploring on foot for devotees of English regional styles. Here we can see three almost indestructible building ma-terials—Mountsorrel granite, Swith-land slate, and Barrow-on-Soar lime-mortar. In a different class is the elegant red-brick vicarage (late 18th century). The church (St Peter) is mostly about 1800 in date, "thor-oughly restored" in 1888; another church (Christ Church) was built in 1844.

Older writers rather despised Mountsorrel, calling it "an unkempt little town"—and so it is—but it is a fascinating place all the same. There are nice views of it from the other side of the Soar. A bridge crossed the river here as early as the 13th century, but the present iron bridge

MOUNTSORREL

Slate headstones, NARBOROUGH

dates from 1860. The river is canalised here (Grand Union Canal) and as late as the 1930s boats left Jelly's Wharf frequently "to any part of the Kingdom".

Mowsley (8) has much decent 18th-century red-brick building, and pleasant scenery all round. The church (St Nicholas) is aisleless and cruciform, with north and south transepts, all built about 1300. Restored by J. L. Pearson in 1882. The main altar is the original medieval stone slab. Some wainscotting in the south transept comes from the old hall at Knaptoft (*q.v.*).

Muston (3) lies in the vale of Belvoir.

The church (St John the Baptist) is mostly 13th–14th century in date, as witness the Early English nave arcades and the Decorated west tower. Some late medieval bench-ends remain. George Crabbe (1754–1832) was rector here 1789–1814 but absent most of the time. He was recalled to his duties by the bishop in 1805 and finally left after his wife's death. He was chaplain to the Duke of Rutland at Belvoir 1782–5, and wrote *The Village* while there. Unpopular at Muston, they rang the bells for his successor before he left for good. The duke presented him to Trowbridge in Wiltshire, where he resided, a happier man, until his death in 1832.

Nailstone (4) is a large colliery village, with the usual brickworks attached. The charmingly named village of Barton-in-the-Beans is in this parish also. Here the Deacons have been clock and watch makers for several generations. Nailstone church (All Saints) is the usual 13th- to 14th-century Leicestershire type, notable for its spacious interior. It was restored by Ewan Christian in 1853; the tower and spire were restored in 1898.

Narborough (7) is a large village, mostly modern and depressing, but the old main street has several attractive 18th-century houses which one comes to regard as "typical

NEVILL HOLT

Leicestershire". Entering the village from the west one sees a large stone-built house of *c.* 1600, evidently the old manor house. The church (All Saints) has a 15th-century tower, nave, and aisles, with a chancel of 1887. The whole building is over-restored and devoid of interest. In the churchyard, however, is a very good collection of Swithland slate headstones, ranging in date from the early 18th to the early 19th century: *see* especially the series to the Billson family.

Nether Broughton (5). A large village below the escarpment of the Leicester-shire wolds. Some good houses, e.g. Heckadeck Cottage, dated 1762. Ironstone church (St Mary) on edge of village, indeed really outside it. Beautifully situated with Vale of Belvoir in front and the wolds be-hind: views from the churchyard on a summer afternoon. Mostly 13th–

14th-century church, over-restored in 1841 but still a pleasant interior because of the colour of the iron-stone. A fragment of a pre-Conquest stone in the vestry is only of mild antiquarian interest.

Nevill Holt (9) stands on a hill-top with fine views of the Welland valley and the Northamptonshire uplands beyond. It began as a clearing in the woods in the 12th and 13th centuries, but is now little more than the hall and church. The old village decayed when the open fields were enclosed for sheep and cattle pastures in the late 15th century or the early 16th. The hall, now a preparatory school, is a splendid medieval house of many periods but starting about 1400. Much of the building was done by Thomas Palmer (d. 1474), and added to by Sir Thomas Nevill between 1591 and 1636. There were later altera-tions also, notably an extensive

"Gothicisation" by Papworth in 1829–32. The stables are late 17th century.

From 1876 to 1912 the estate was owned by the great shipping family of Cunard, and played a considerable part in the hunting and social history of Leicestershire and beyond. The hall became a school in 1919.

The church (St Mary) is physically almost part of the hall. It is mainly late 13th century in date, but the font of *c.* 1150 survives from an older church. As so often happened, the church was heightened in the 15th century and given Perpendicular windows throughout. Finely-carved Jacobean pulpit. Nevill monuments in the south transept, notably that of Sir Thomas Nevill, 1636.

Hall Farm is an unaltered late 17th-century farmhouse.

Newbold Verdon (4) takes its second name from Bertram de Verdon, who

86

held the manor in the time of Stephen (1135–54). The church (St James) was "repaired and enlarged" in 1832, and rebuilt (all but the tower) in 1899. The hall, a good late 17th-century house, was lived in for a time by Nathaniel Crew, bishop of Durham (1633–1721) and also by Lady Mary Wortley Montagu (1689–1762). The famous "blue-stocking" wrote of it in 1744 as "one of the most charming and pleasant places I ever saw. The gardens are delightful, the park very beautiful, the house neat and agreeable, and everything about it is in elegant taste."

Newton Harcourt (8) is a small village on the banks of the Grand Union Canal, again a favourite place for walkers and fishermen. The little church (St Luke) is rather disappointing. The tower is the original 13th-century work but the remainder of the church has been thoroughly Victorianised. Nearby is the attractive manor house, probably built in the late 16th century and perhaps added to in the early 17th.

Newtown Linford (4), the favourite way into Bradgate Park, was once a pretty little "Forest village" with a good deal of interesting old building, especially examples of cruck cottages. These are still here, but much else has invaded the old village in the past 10 or 20 years. The church (All Saints) was pretty heavily renewed in 1860 and again in 1893 (chancel and north transept). The most attractive feature, as Pevsner says, is the 18th-century tympanum bearing the royal arms of George III.

Normanton-le-Heath (4), perilously near the coalfield, has a pretty Decorated church (Holy Trinity), all of the 14th century—though the font may be earlier, and the simple screen is Perpendicular. The village stands high by Leicestershire standards and there are extensive views towards the rugged hills of Charnwood, and southwards over the placid (even rather dull) countryside of west Leicestershire. Much of the parish was a large, open heath—as the name implies—until it was enclosed in 1629.

North Kilworth (8) is "an irregularly built village" not far from the Grand Union Canal. The church (St Andrew) is mainly of 14th-century date, the chancel excellent and somewhat earlier; the south aisle and arcade date from 1864, when the church was over-restored. The Belgraves have lived in the parish since the 14th century, and provided rectors here from 1701 to 1901, with only a short break from 1804–12. In the chancel is a brass memorial to a young Capt. Belgrave (1896–1918) with a typical "biography" of a young man in the First World War. Belgraves still reside in the parish. The list of rectors in the church—always something one should read when provided—shows that Archbishop Laud was rector in 1608–9, though it is doubtful whether he ever resided in his benefice: two years later he was elected President of St John's College, Oxford, and thence began his meteoric ascent to high offices.

Norton by Twycross (1) has a church (Holy Trinity) originally built c. 1300 but so restored as to be of no interest.

Noseley (9), set deep in hilly and wooded country, some of the most beautiful in Leicestershire, is now only a hall and a private chapel. The village, which stood just northwest of the present park, decayed when the Hazleriggs converted the open fields to pastures in the early 16th century, but the site is still prominent on the ground.

The hall was rebuilt on a much older site in the 1720s. The Hazleriggs acquired Noseley by marriage about 1435 and are still here, having come south from the depths of Northumberland (just like the Manners family, now dukes of Rutland. *See* under *Belvoir*).

There was a church here before 1081, but it was already in decay by the 1330s and the free chapel took over. This was built in the late 13th century, the side-walls raised in the 15th, and a crenellated parapet added. The present interior arrangements reflect the collegiate character of the original foundation. The ornate stalls date from c. 1473–4; Elizabethan or Jacobean panelling on the east wall; screen; much medieval stained glass; numerous Hazlerigg monuments and incised slabs.

Oadby (8) today is neither a village nor a town. No doubt the sociologists will coin some dreadful word for this kind of agglomeration in time. There is only one thing to see in the whole place, the parish church (St Peter), and even this was heavily restored in the 1880s. Generally speaking the church was built 1300–30 but the arcades and clerestory are Perpendicular. Good west tower and broach spire.

Some of the Halls of Residence of the University of Leicester are technically in Oadby. Two of them are interesting examples of rich men's Tudor of the early 20th century.

Archaeologically, Oadby is much more interesting, though there is nothing to see. An important pagan Anglo-Saxon cemetery was found on the edge of the village in the time of George III, and in the 1950s the building of modern houses led to the discovery of Roman pottery and a few burials and also fragments of an Anglo-Saxon urn. The archaeologists find it difficult to know what to make of this site, but it could represent an important example of continuity from the Romano–British period into the Anglo-Saxon.

Old Dalby (5) is sometimes called Dalby-on-the-Wolds, (i.e. Wold Dalby). It is beautifully situated below the escarpment of the wolds and embosomed in trees. The village has long been noted for its fine Stilton cheese which is still made here. The church (St John) is a dull building, the old church having been pulled down in 1834 and the present one built in 1835 and restored in 1894. The only things of interest in the church are three tombs of 16th- to early 17th-century date which are behind the reredos and are reached by a separate door from the outside. These are the tomb of Andrew Noel, Esq., 1562, and his two wives; another tomb to Sir Andrew Noel, 1603; and a miniature tomb with three recumbent effigies—Thomas Hopton, Esq., and his wife and her second husband, Sir Thomas Tyrrell. Pevsner gives c. 1580 for this curious little tomb.

Dalby Hall was described as a large stone mansion in 1846.

Orton-on-the-Hill (1) lies on the extreme west of Leicestershire, overlooking Warwickshire, more than 300 ft. up, a considerable height for these parts. The church (St Edith) is mostly Decorated in style, but remodelled in the Perpendicular period. It should be seen for its furnishings and architectural details, including a rare effigy of a Cistercian abbot in the north aisle. Orton Hall dates from the late 18th century and was described in 1846 as "a neat mansion with pleasant grounds" occupied by the Rev. D. Steele Perkins. In the reign of Charles II the manor was bought by the Steeles, whose heiress carried it by marriage to the Perkins family.

Osbaston (4) is a small village near Market Bosworth with no church. The church was destroyed long ago. The hall in parts is 16th to 17th century but was pretty well rebuilt in 1750 with a handsome south front. For a long time it was in a decaying state, but was sold in May 1967 and is now being brought back to life.

Osgathorpe (4) has a 14th-century church (St Mary) with pleasing north and south windows to the nave and chancel. Though the church was over-restored in Victorian days, the interior is more appealing than one would suspect, and there is a particularly attractive sanctuary, all well cared for.

Opposite the church is an unusual village school, built in 1670, with almshouses of the same date, quite striking in this otherwise undistinguished village. There is also a good example of a 16th-century yeoman farmer's house just south-west of the church, with a beautiful Swithland slate roof.

Owston (6) (pronounced Ooston) lies deep in the heart of the Leicestershire uplands, rising to more than 600 ft. in the south part of the parish. Far from any main road, it is a countryside of footpaths and bridle roads, little streams and ancient woods. An Augustinian abbey was founded here shortly before 1161, though little remains of it except the present parish church which represents a part of the abbey church. Just southwest of the village are a pond and earthworks which probably represent the fish-ponds of the old abbey.

The church (St Andrew) is rather difficult to unravel. Pevsner says it represents the chancel of the abbey church with a wide chapel, but it is more likely to be part of the nave. Post-Reformation changes, together with 18th- and 19th-century restorations have made the building history too dubious, but certainly the chancel was said to be "ruined" in 1556 and it was probably demolished soon after. The nave roof was heightened *c.* 1500 and the abbey was dissolved in 1539. Of the original 12th-century building all that remains is a blocked south doorway and a north doorway.

Owston village is very much smaller than it was in medieval times, when a record of 1348 speaks of 35 houses let by the abbey. Out in the parish are two small sites of deserted villages—Newbold, about 1 mile north-west of Owston, is now only a farm but was formerly a village with its own little church in the 12th century; North Marefield, also called Old Marefield, is another lost village, the site being just west of the minor road from South Marefield to Burrough-on-the-Hill. Old Marefield also had a little church by 1166, but the whole site had been depopulated before 1500.

Packington (4) formerly had a weekly market and an annual fair like so many Leicestershire villages in the Middle Ages. The church (Holy Rood) is 13th century, "repaired and enlarged in 1843", and it is this later work that gives the character today. Village lock-up, as at Breedon, Worthington, and elsewhere.

Peatling Magna (8). A large village in pleasant country with an interesting church (All Saints), mostly 13th century though the south doorway would seem to be *c.* 1180–1200. There were the usual Perpendicular improvements: see for example the early 16th-century windows in the chancel. The battlements were added after 1485, as witnessed by the Tudor rose on the corbel table. This prob-

ably dates the late Perpendicular windows also. The contents of the church are of more than usual interest. The benches in the nave are probably all of 1604, a date which appears on one of them; others have initials. The pulpit, with its canopy, is of 1685. The roof of the nave is mostly original medieval work. In the vestry are the remains of the 15th-century screen. Founder's tomb in the north wall of the chancel, a fine example of early 13th-century work with dog-toothed ornament. There are 16th-century tombs to the Jervis family who started as yeomen in Henry VIII's time and raised themselves in two or three generations to be the local squires.

Peatling Parva (8) lies in the attractive upland country of south Leicestershire. The church (St Andrew) has been terribly over-restored (1870) but the triple chancel arch of this date is remarkably successful. Almost covered by the altar table is an incised slab to William Bradgate (d. 1480), a big farmer characteristic of this age of rising yeomen who grew rich enough to buy the lordship of the manor in later years and remained thereafter as squires for several generations.

The hall, near by, is a Queen Anne building, altered in the 1840s but still handsome.

Peckleton (7) is a small village right on the Roman road from Leicester to *Manduessedum*, a posting station on Watling Street. It may have been an early site in the English settlement, as the name probably embodies the folk-name "Peohtla's people". The church (St Mary, not St Martin as Pevsner says) stands on a hill well outside the village and immediately raises the problem of why this site was chosen. Indeed, it suggests that it is an ancient site and was chosen for that reason. The approach is up a very stony track which seems to have had little done to it from the Middle Ages, but there is a less interesting and more practicable way up further down the village. The 14th-century church is in great need of repair but being slowly rescued, and it could be

NOSELEY, 15th-century woodcarving

a very appealing building when it is finished. Decorated west tower and slender crocketed spire, spacious chancel with a good east window (glass by Kempe). The font is probably 12th century. There are a few interesting monuments including two early 14th-century effigies (one civilian, the other a knight and his lady). There is also a memorial to Dr Robert Chessher (1750–1831), a distinguished surgeon who was born at Peckleton and is buried here in the churchyard. He practised at Hinckley and was celebrated for the cure of spinal diseases.

The hall is just south of the church, rather grand late Georgian and now empty and acquiring a look of decay. There is a medieval moated site on the low ground south of the village.

Pickwell (6) is a small village high on the marlstone uplands, with much attractive ironstone building. The manor house is early 17th century and onwards in date. Leesthorpe is in this parish. The old village was deserted at some date, and the site can be seen from the Melton–Oakham main road just east of Leesthorpe Hall. It was partly unearthed during the Second World War. Pickwell church (All Saints) existed in the 11th century, but nothing remains from this early period: the oldest surviving evidence is the Norman font. The nave is possibly of this date also, as the north arcade is early 13th

century, the south arcade c. 1300. Much rebuilding took place in the early 14th century, e.g. the chancel with its tall Decorated windows, and the pretty little clerestory to the nave (an unusual date for this feature). In the early 15th century the handsome tower was added, built of a fine ash-lar limestone in contrast to the old-gold ironstone of the body of the church.

Dr William Cave, the ecclesiastical historian and chaplain to Charles II, was born at the rectory 30 December 1637, during his father's incumbency of Pickwell.

Plungar (3) is a large village in the Vale of Belvoir with a church (St Helen) which was enlarged and restored in the 1850s. It contains, however, a number of late medieval bench ends.

Potters Marston (7) is one of the numerous sites of "lost villages" in Leicestershire. The site of the village was in Big Township Close where pottery kilns were found during war-time ploughing-up. It was called Potters Marston by 1251, so clearly it was already the centre of a local industry. The site of the village and the kilns is in the field immediately east of the chapel across the moat.

The chapel (St Mary) consists of nave and chancel with plain mul-lioned windows, all rather difficult to date. The hall is partly medieval,

partly early 18th century, and there is Jacobean work inside.

Prestwold (5) is now only a big house and a church; the village has dis-appeared. The hall is mostly an 18th-century house, enlarged and re-faced in the 1840s in a restrained classical style. The estate still be-longs to the Packes, who bought it in 1650. The purchaser was Sir Christopher Packe, Lord Mayor of London 1654–5, a strong partisan of Cromwell who proposed in 1656 that Cromwell should assume the title of king. He was disqualified at the Restoration from holding any public office. Nevertheless, the Packes flourished and in Victorian days lorded it over more than 6,000 acres in Leicestershire and Lincolnshire.

The church (St Andrew) is in the grounds of the hall. It is locked but the key is kept at the hall. It has a Perpendicular west tower but the rest is a late Victorian restoration by Blomfield, and the only notable feature is the Packe monuments ranging from 1682 to 1946. The monument of 1682 is to Sir Christopher Packe who bought the estate originally. The monument to Charles James Packe of Prestwold, esquire, tells us that he succeeded his father in 1735 and died in 1816 after enjoying his inheritance for no less than 81 years. There is also a monu-ment dated 1631 to Sir William Skipwith, a previous owner of the manor, and an alabaster monument to two ladies *c.* 1520 (Pevsner). These two ladies are traditionally said to have been the builders of Swarkston Bridge.

Quenby (5) was once an upland village but was depopulated in the late 15th century. Unlike many of these sites, this one is very difficult to find on the ground. It is in the park of the great house, Quenby Hall, one of the finest houses in the county, built about 1621–36 in brick on an "H" plan. The interior, which is not usually shown to the public, is of the highest interest and contains most of its original features.

Queniborough (5) is an attractive village with many good houses of 17th-century to early 19th-century date. The church (St Mary) is notable for a superb tower and needle-like spire. Norman chancel, 13th-century arcades to the nave, but the present aisles are Decorated work of the early 14th century. The usual Perpendicular clerestory and roof, and a screen of the same date.

Quorndon (5), a large village on the edge of Charnwood Forest, has a great deal of interesting vernacular building and repays a leisurely walk round it. Quorndon House, now an 1820 house, has been the seat of the Farnhams since 1284, and they are still there. At Quorndon Hall, a house of *c.* 1680, much altered but with a fine staircase of that date, lived the famous Hugo Meynell (from 1750). He founded the Quorn Hunt here, which has ever since been the summit of English fox-hunting society. The hall now belongs to the Loughborough University.

The church (St Bartholomew) is mainly an early 14th-century building, but some Norman work remains (south doorway, and priest's doorway). The tower is Perpendicular, the north aisle dates from 1842. The Farnham Chapel contains several monuments to the family, most notably that of John Farnham, 1587.

Ragdale (5) lies in a small valley in the gentle wolds of north Leicestershire. The village was once very decayed indeed and almost dis-

appeared, but has revived in recent years and is larger than ever. The church (All Saints) is beautifully sited within a golden ironstone wall, rather like a miniature medieval city. It is mostly rustic work of the 14th century with a low west tower (Perpendicular) repaired in old brick. There is a diminutive 15th-century clerestory and the whole building is of worn ironstone in a state of pleasing decay. The interior is minute. It is clearly a church built mostly with peasant money, unlike the grand church at Stoke Golding (*q.v.*) which was built by the local squire about the same time.

Ragdale Old Hall was built by Sir Henry Shirley in 1629–30 and included part of an earlier half-timbered house. The *Little Guide* says "the combination of the warm brick, grey stone and timber with the rich orange of the adjacent church makes a delightful picture". Alas, the Old Hall was unforgivably demolished in 1958. The New Hall was built some distance away in 1785 and castellated in the early 19th century. There are beautiful views to the south from the Hoby road, looking across the Wreak Valley to Billesdon Coplow.

Ratby (4) has a nice, mainly Decorated church (St Philip and St James) with particularly beautiful traceried windows. The tower is Early English (lower stage) and so is the south arcade, but nave, south aisle, and chancel are all early 19th century. So also is the font. Note the unfinished carving on one capital in the nave—possibly work interrupted by the Black Death (1349) and never completed.

Bury Camp, about a mile west of the village, is a well-preserved Roman earthwork, perhaps a military camp made in connection with the building of the Fosse Way 5 miles behind. If so, it is mid-1st century in date.

Old Hays is one of the best-preserved moated homestead sites in the county, but the house on the island was rebuilt in 1733.

Ratcliffe Culey (1) gets its odd second name from the Culeys who were lords of the manor in the 13th century. The original Culey is in Normandy. Near the church is a considerable moated

site where the manor house once stood. The church (All Saints) is attractive, entirely Decorated in style, with good detail everywhere inside.

Ratcliffe-on-the-Wreak (5) has a pleasant church (St Botolph) of mostly early 14th-century date, the font probably about 1200. Ratcliffe Hall is Georgian. Shipley Hill was long thought to be a great burial mound but is now considered to be a natural formation, as Earl Ferrers surmised as long ago as the 18th century. The Roman Catholic College, begun in 1843, is largely the work of A. W. Pugin, completed by Hansom. It was the first R.C. college to be founded in England since the Reformation. Note, too, the old mill on the River Wreak, on the road to Rearsby.

Ravenstone (4). Fine Early Georgian hall (*c.* 1725) with two wings added in 1844–5. The church (St Michael) is mainly *c.* 1300. Most remarkable are the almshouses founded in 1711. They cover a large area and were not finally completed until 1814.

Rearsby (5) is now considerably overgrown, like most villages within the orbit of Leicester, but the old village along the brook is pleasant and has "several neat houses" as the old Directories would say. There is also a medieval bridge of six arches over the stream. The church (St Michael) has an ashlar Perpendicular tower, but the body of the building is probably 13th century. The south arcade is of this date and the north arcade is 14th century. The chancel was rebuilt in the Perpendicular period and the font is 13th century.

Redmile (3) has fine views of Belvoir Castle and the miles of woods along the escarpment. Its name means "red mould" (i.e. soil). The church (St Peter) has a crocketed spire and an over-restored exterior, but the interior is more pleasing than one would expect—Decorated south arcade and in the chancel a nice collection of poppyhead benches (late medieval). Just beyond the church is the now derelict Nottingham and Grantham Canal, closed down in 1929. The old canal wharf is now a car park. One of the rectors of Redmile was the Rev. Thomas Daffy, who resided here from 1666 until his death in 1680. He is known to fame as the inventor of Daffy's "Elixir", a popular cure for all fleshly ills in the 18th century. His daughter carried on after his death, but his elixir was eventually superseded by another miracle cure called "James's Powder".

"DAFFY'S ELIXIR"

"a certain Cure (under God) in most Distempers, viz. The Gout and Rheumatism, with all those torturing Pains attending them; it takes away the Scurvy, Root and Branch, and gives immediate Ease in the most Racking Pains of the Cholick. It's a Sovereign and never failing Remedy against Fluxes, spitting of Blood, Consumption, Agues, Small Pox, and Meazles; it carries off the most violent Fevers; it eases After-Pains, and prevents Miscarriages; cures the Rickets in Children; Is wonderful in the Stone, and Gravel in the Kidneys, Bladder or Ureter, and brings away Slime, Gravel, and oftentimes Stones of a great Bigness. For Stoppage or Pains in the Stomach, Shortness of Breath, Pains in the Head and Heart, a better Remedy in the World cannot be. It perfectly destroy Worms, tho' you are almost overgrown with them; cureth the black or yellow Jaundice, King's Evil, and those who are stopp'd with Flegm, restoring a languishing Body to perfect Health, strengthening the Vessels of both Sexes, and changeth the whole Mass of Blood, being a noble Cordial after hard Drinking."

Rolleston (9) lies in very attractive secluded country in south-east Leicestershire. The hall was "a handsome stone mansion newly fronted about 1700" but was demolished in 1955 and a smaller house in the Tudor style built on the site. The little church (St John) was mostly rebuilt in 1740 but the 13th-century tower was left as it was. The whole church has been pleasantly restored in recent years and has now a decent plain interior. Queen Victoria is said to have presented the harmonium to the church.

Rotherby (5) is one of the many Danish villages in the valley of the Wreak, deriving its name from a red-haired Dane "*Hradi's by*". It is a very pleasant and well-kept village with pastoral views across the river valley from the churchyard, tree-shaded roads, and 18th-century red-brick cottages with Swithland slate roofs. The church (All Saints) is almost entirely a Decorated building with a Perpendicular tower at the end of the south aisle, and a pretty Decorated clerestory. Note the blocked 12th-century window in the west wall of the nave, evidence of an earlier building.

Rothley (5), a large village on the eastern edge of Charnwood, is popular with the well-to-do commuters of neighbouring Leicester. The old village has much good vernacular building, including a remarkable number of cruck-framed cottages of late medieval to 16th-century date.

The church (St Mary and St John the Baptist) is impressive, though much restored outside, with a re-built chancel (1878). Apart from the Norman font, the interior is nearly all early 14th century in date. Screen, and various monuments running from 1486 onwards. Good Swithland slate headstones in churchyard, and also a fine pre-Conquest cross— probably *c*. 850 in date.

Rothley Temple gets its name from the Knights Templars, to whom it once belonged. The late 13th-century chapel is the best surviving work of their time. The house is a mixture of medieval, Elizabethan, and 1890s (rebuilt south wing). Thomas Babington Macaulay (1800–59), the Victorian historian, was born here 25 October 1800, when it was the seat of Thomas Babington, his father's brother-in-law. When he was raised to the peerage in 1857 he took the title of Baron Macaulay of Rothley.

Saddington (8) is a pleasant hill-top village in very attractive country, especially to the east and south. Here the last factory village has been left behind and the wind blows straight

SAXBY

92

from the Northamptonshire uplands, sweeping away the vapours of
industrial Leicester. The village contains several pleasant houses of early
19th-century date, but the church (St
Helen) was virtually rebuilt in 1872–3
except the tower and the nave arcades.
The south arcade is 13th century, the
oldest part of the church.

The Grand Union Canal flows, if
that is the right word, on the east and
north-eastern edge of the parish and
provides some favourite walking and
coarse fishing. It passes through
Saddington Tunnel, about half a mile
long, made in 1797. Apart from this,
there are miles of car-free walking
along the towpath in both directions.

Saltby (6) lies high up towards the
Lincolnshire border. The church (St
Peter) is isolated from the small
village just like that at Sproxton.
It has a 13th-century tower to which
a Perpendicular top stage has been
added. The interior is an austere
Perpendicular one. There are good
medieval corbel faces to the nave
roof. The chancel is rebuilt Victorian.

Not far away on Saltby Heath are
the mysterious earthworks known as
King Lud's Entrenchments. They
probably date from the Dark Ages
and were perhaps a boundary between two kingdoms. The tradition
is that a King Lud was buried at one
end: certainly there was a King of
Mercia called Ludeca who was
killed in battle in 827, and it may
well be that his name is perpetuated
in this form.

Sapcote (7) has a few nice houses in
the old centre of the village which
was once famous for some of the
best cheese in the county, i.e. Leicester
cheese as distinct from Stilton.

The church (All Saints) was once
Decorated and Perpendicular but, as
Pevsner says, has been "severely
ruined". There is, however, a very
fine Norman font. In the vicarage
garden are the remains of a castle
which was once the home of the
great medieval family of Basset from
the 12th century onwards.

Saxby (6) now bears a Scandinavian
name, but the discovery of a large
Anglo-Saxon cemetery here shows
that the Old English were here before
the Danes. The church (St Peter) was

SHEARSBY

entirely rebuilt in 1789 by George
Richardson, who also built Stapleford church. As Pevsner says, "It is
an attempt at combining the tradition
of the Hawksmoor churches of
London with Leicestershire usage".
The interior is plain and decent, as
one would expect. The neighbouring
rectory is of the same date.

Saxelby (5) is a picturesque but un-

tidy village with many ironstone
farmhouses. The church (St Peter)
is the usual mixture in this district
of brilliant ironstone with limestone
dressings. The tower and crocketed
spire are Perpendicular. Again the
body of the church is mostly 13th
century with a clerestory added
c. 1500 when the chancel was also
rebuilt, but unfortunately rebuilt
again in 1856. The font and pulpit

are both good examples of their time, i.e. *c.* 1500, when the church was much improved, but the late medieval benches mentioned in the *Little Guide* disappeared more than 20 years ago. The painting in the church is by Bernardo Strozzi— "The Tribute Money".

Scalford (6). The name means "shallow ford." In 1303 the village had a fair and a weekly market. The church: St Egelwin the Martyr is the curious dedication. It is possible it is Edwin, King and Martyr, though the dedication is sometimes said to be to St Martin. It stands on a fine bold site on an eminence above the village and is basically a 13th-century church with two Early English arcades. The fine west tower was rebuilt in 1649 and the chancel in 1845. Goldsmith Grange, one mile south-east of the village, is named after one John Goldsmith, a merchant of Melton Mowbray who flourished *c.* 1400 and bought much land hereabouts.

Scraptoft (5) stands on rising ground on the eastern edge of Leicester, much less spoilt than most of the peripheral villages. The church (All Saints) is "typical" of east Leicestershire, i.e. ironstone fabric with limestone dressings, and all built round about 1300. The font is Early English. Some minor monuments to the Wigleys, who lived at the adjacent hall. The latter, now a College of Education, is a handsome early 18th-century house with a Tudor core. Nether Hall is dated 1709, of brick with Swithland slate roof.

Seagrave (5) is a large village at the western end of the Leicestershire wolds. The Fosse Way (A.46) lies along the eastern edge of the parish. The church (All Saints) is typical Leicestershire in period and style, i.e. a Perpendicular tower with a nave of 13th to 14th century and a chancel rebuilt in 1891. The font is Norman.

Sewstern (6) is a small village just west of the ancient drove road, here the county boundary between

Leicestershire and Lincolnshire, which goes for miles as Sewstern Lane, or The Drift. The church (Holy Trinity) is by Salvin, 1842, and replaced an ancient church long ago demolished. There is ironstone working on a large scale all round here.

Shackerstone (4) lies near the Ashby-de-la-Zouch Canal. The church (St Peter), as so often happened in Leicestershire, was rebuilt in the Victorian period except the Perpendicular tower.

Shangton (8), a small and secluded village in the beautiful unspoilt country of south-east Leicestershire.

SOUTH CROXTON

The church (St Nicholas) is built of rubble ironstone masonry and is largely unrestored 14th-century work, except the chancel, which was rebuilt in 1873. Some original 14th-century windows but also several square-headed Perpendicular windows—attractive rustic work—inserted *c.* 1500. The only monument of any note is to Sir Matthew Saunders, 1623. Francis Saunders bought the manor in 1560, and the little manor house near the church was probably built by his son Matthew. In the churchyard are some good Ketton headstones, some of them late 17th century, which is about the earliest period at which headstones appear in churchyards.

12th-century font at
SOUTH CROXTON

SPROXTON

Sharnford (7) is an elongated and rather depressing village on the busy main road from Leicester to Coventry. The church (St Helen) is of little interest, having been too well restored at the usual time.

Shawell (8). The church (All Saints) is entirely of 1865–6, except the Perpendicular tower. Near it is a large moated site.

Shearsby (8), amid attractive hilly country in south Leicestershire, has little else to commend it. The church (St Mary Magdalene) has a tower rebuilt in 1789, but the rest of the building was most unfortunately restored and is of no interest. Close to the church is a fine example of a yeoman's house which was for years falling into ruin but is now (1968)

being rescued and brought back to life. It used to carry the date 1669, but I suspect it was in fact a considerably older building and this date may have referred to a later repair.

Sheepy Magna (1) has a dark and dull church (All Saints). The nave was rebuilt in 1789 and robbed of its brasses and subsequently heavily Victorianised. There are, however, four windows in the nave of great interest, two by Burne-Jones, of 1879, and two by Kempe, 1897. The neighbouring village of Sheepy Parva is notable chiefly for a large mill with a very picturesque mill-pond on the River Sence. This is an old mill site. In 1846 it was described as "a large water and steam mill".

Shenton (7) is notable chiefly for the fine hall, dated 1629, and built of brick with stone dressings. The church was entirely rebuilt in 1862.

Shepshed (4) is a huge, formless village with a biggish market place as a central feature; presumably there was a market here from medieval times and also a fair. The church (St Botolph) stands on the top of a hill leading out of the village, and indeed it looks as though it is built on the top of a gigantic mound. If so, I suspect that this Christian church was deliberately built on a pre-Christian place of worship. The present church has a 13th-century tower with a dumpy broach spire and a certain amount of 15th-century work inside. The nave roof is dated 1652, but as a whole the interior

96

seems not only Victorianised but rather formless, like the village, owing to the frequent changes. The nave contains, however, some good late medieval benches with poppy heads. There are a number of monuments of the Phillipps family of Garendon, mostly of 18th- or 19th-century dates.

In the village the Roman Catholic church is by Pugin (1842), and there is a good deal of vernacular building worth looking at if one walks around the numerous little streets and lanes. Pevsner also rightly draws attention to the Westminster Bank which he calls "a monstrosity of brick and buff terra-cotta", built in 1903. Since it is built in terra-cotta, age cannot wither it nor the years condemn. It may indeed be a bit of a show-piece in a hundred years' time.

Shoby (5) was formerly an independent parish and village, but the village was abandoned long ago and the church has also disappeared. The Ordnance Survey map used to mark "remains of priory", but there was never a priory here and the reference is probably to the remains of the ruined parish church. Priory Farm contains a certain amount of old work, mostly about 1600, and is probably the cut-down remains of Lady Englefield's great house. The village site is probably in the field on either side of the drive into Priory Farm.

Sibson (4) was once a much larger village than it is today and contains a few attractive houses. Most notable is The Cock Inn, a well-preserved timber-framed house of the early 17th century. The church (St Botolph) has an 18th-century stone-built tower with an 18th-century brick nave, all done in the Classical style in 1726. Unfortunately, the restoration in 1872 spoilt what must have been a very attractive Georgian interior. The early 14th-century chancel escaped the 18th-century rebuilding but was much restored at a later date. However, there is a good triple sedilia and an

STAPLEFORD: monument by Rysbrack

effigy of a 14th-century woman: also an excellent brass of John Moore, rector (d. 1532), in priest's vestments. Note the medieval nave roof and note also that among the rectors was Thomas Neale, who died in 1859 aged 94 and was rector here for no less than 67 years. The National School was built in 1839, and the first stone was laid by the Queen Dowager Adelaide.

Sileby (5) is one of the unloveliest villages one could find anywhere: a Midland industrial village, red-brick, dreary. The church (St Mary) was built just before and after 1300, mostly early 14th century. The tower is the best feature. Lower part early 14th century, upper Perpendicular, the whole a fine design worthy of Somerset in some respects.

Skeffington (6), a small village over 600 ft. above sea-level in rolling, wooded country, especially towards Launde and Halstead. Pleasant village, mostly ironstone houses and cottages. The church (St Thomas à Becket) is attractive, though it was almost entirely rebuilt in 1860. Decorated arcade, and much Perpendicular work also. Note the corbels in nave, and the roof corbels. Dilapidated Skeffington monuments. They lived at the hall from at least the 13th century, but the present hall is a puzzling mixture of early 17th century, early Georgian, and the 1840s. The whole setting is very picturesque.

Slawston (9) lies amidst beautiful rolling countryside towards Hallaton. It is a secluded village with much pleasant 18th-century building. The church (All Saints) is outside the village. Ironstone tower (Decorated) and a short limestone broach spire. Note the Decorated clerestory with rustic tracery. The church is basically 14th century but the chancel was rebuilt in 1864.

Smeeton Westerby (8) has little of note in it. The church (Christ Church) was built by Woodyer (1852) in the Decorated style. There is pleasing country all round Smeeton, with beautiful views across to the Gumley hills and down to Harborough.

Snarestone (4), a small village with a church (St Bartholomew) built in 1732 with a Victorianised interior. In the village street some good 18th-century houses.

Snibston (4) has an isolated little church (St Mary) of nave and chancel only, built of Forest stone: probably an early 13th-century building, over-restored in Victorian times, and now wholly uninteresting in the interior. The surrounding country is dull and plastered with waste-tips, evidences of the coalfield. George Stephenson and his partners were responsible for building some of the village from 1831 onwards when the colliery got going.

Somerby (6) is a large village, high up on the Leicestershire uplands, with a good deal of local ironstone building and also much unfortunate red-brick. White's *Directory* for 1863 reveals that there was then a "Somerby Association for the Prosecution of Felons" supported by the gentry and farmers of the neighbourhood—an unpleasant air of persecution pervades this title. The church (All Saints) is a bold ironstone building (much worn) with a central ironstone tower and a recessed spire of limestone, all early 14th century in date. The nave is *c.* 1250, with a beautiful north arcade of that date: the south arcade in a similar style is a copy done in the 1860s, when the aisles were much restored. Chancel early 14th century, with triple sedilia and Decorated windows. The font is 13th century, richly and heavily decorated. The simple Norman doorway to the chancel was presumably saved from an earlier church.

Somerby Hall (18th-century) was the home of Col. Fred Burnaby (1842–85) for a time, a mighty traveller in his day, notably in "the ride to Khiva" in 1875. He was killed in the attempt to relieve Khartoum in the Sudan. Another native of Somerby was Sir Benjamin Ward Richardson (1828–96), the eminent physician and apostle of teetotalism (only two cheers for this).

South Croxton (5) (pronounced *Croson*) always seems to me a rather untidy village on a hillside, crowned by a fine church (St John the Baptist) of weathered ironstone—beautiful golden colour and a decayed texture. The ironstone tower has a short limestone spire, as is characteristic of so many Leicestershire churches in these parts. The whole church was built in the first half of the 14th century: good Decorated work throughout and almost unspoilt, conservatively restored, 1936–8. Norman font on a 14th-century base. The spacious interior has been cleared of all unnecessary furniture so that the Decorated proportions are clearly revealed. The 14th-century roof has been replaced by a Perpendicular one which shows the considerable remains of the original principals and medieval figures above the corbels. Eighteenth-century pulpit. Altogether a very good country interior, complete with the brick and tiled floor.

Good moated site north of the church, and considerable traces of the old village site to the north-west.

South Kilworth (8), a large village with some good houses and an interesting church (St Nicholas). Late Norman north arcade and font. Restored by Bodley, 1869. Fine Tudor yeoman's house west of the church. Medieval moated site just south of the village, with fish-ponds.

Sproxton (6) is pronounced *Sproson*. The church (St Bartholomew) stands high, far outside the village to the north, and is therefore possibly an ancient site. It has an Anglo-Saxon cross in the churchyard (10th century), the only complete cross of its kind in the county. The west tower is 13th-century ironstone to which a top stage has been added in the 14th century. The south arcade is *c.* 1300, but on the whole the interior has been much restored. There are wide views from the churchyard. Possibly the cross preceded any church on this site.

Stanford (8) is divided by the Avon between Leicestershire and Northamptonshire, the hall being in the former county. (*See* the *Shell Guide to Northamptonshire* for the church and village.) The hall, in a beautiful park, was built 1697–1700, and is remarkably fine. Stables of 1737. The house is open to the public and has *inter alia* a good main staircase of 1730.

Stapleford (6), only a hall and a church remain in a large park, the village having disappeared as a result of enclosures for pasture round about 1500. The site of the village is in the park.

The hall, open to the public on certain days, has a complicated building history, the most obvious parts being a wing of 1633, and a main block of about 1680. But the wing was only "repayred" in 1633

and may contain work of *c.* 1500—the original house built by Thomas Sherard—though, as Pevsner says, it is not very clear what was done in 1633 except to "Gothicise" something older. The main part of the house was gone over again in the 1890s. There is now a Lion Reserve in the park.

The church (St Mary Magdalen) was rebuilt in 1783 by George Richardson for the fourth Earl of Harborough (as the Sherards had become). It is completely charming inside, with a ribbed ceiling and pretty west gallery, and all the original fittings arranged as in a college chapel: in all an outstanding

example of 18th-century Gothic. Several Sherard monuments, most notable that of the first earl of Harborough by Rysbrack, 1732, making a superb group with Lady Harborough and her infant child.

Stapleford Park has a place in railway history, when the seventh Lord Harborough's army fought the contractor's army to prevent the Syston and Peterborough railway from running anywhere near his park (1846). There were many battles with the surveyors and the engineers; the sweeping curve of the line round the edge of the park is still known as "Lord Harborough's Curve".

Stapleton (7) has very little of note. The small church (St Martin) dates from about 1300, but is much over-restored. The village, however, had its one moment of fame. On the low ground to the south, called The Bradshaws, King Richard III camped from 18 to 21 August 1485 while he waited for the news of the whereabouts of Henry Earl of Richmond who was then at Atherstone on Watling Street. On Sunday evening, 21 August, Richard moved to Ambion Hill, probably along the footpath that still runs past a moated site towards Sutton Cheney and hence to the fatal battlefield the next day.

Stathern (3) is beautifully sited at the foot of the wooded escarpment with fine views from the hills above. It formerly had a lace manufacture. The church (St Guthlac) is of the usual warm ironstone, mostly late 13th century with a 14th-century west tower and a good 14th-century font. The rectory is large, stylish, 18th-century ironstone. We are in ducal country here.

Staunton Harold (4)—park and lakes, hall and church, nothing else. The village has gone. Called Staunton after all the limestone hereabouts, and Harold after a 12th-century lord of the manor. The manor came to the Shirleys by marriage in 1423. They were afterwards the Earls Ferrers. The Palladian hall, with a superb

STAUNTON HAROLD church interior (see also back endpaper)

STAUNTON HAROLD gate

background of hanging woods and wild heath, was built and designed by the fifth Earl Ferrers from 1763 onwards, though behind the north front the Jacobean mansion was retained, itself altered about 1700. Various fine rooms reflect each of these major periods of alteration. The Ferrers sold the estate in 1954, but the hall was later taken over as a Cheshire Home and saved from demolition.

The church (Holy Trinity) is unique in having been rebuilt in Cromwellian times—begun 1653 and finished in 1665—and in retaining all its original fittings. The woodwork above all is quite remarkable. Also, a fine early 18th-century ironwork screen, probably commissioned by the Robert Shirley whose monument (1714) is near by. Ceiling paintings, 1655.

Pevsner rightly says that the setting of Staunton Harold—great house, church, and park—is unsurpassed in England for its complete Englishness. The hall, grounds, and church are always open to the public.

Like Sir Robert Shirley, who built the church in bad times, Group-Captain Leonard Cheshire, V.C., saved the great house in our own time. They both "did the best things in the worst times and hoped them in the most calamitous"—as the inscription over the west door of the church says of its own time.

Stockerston (9), only the church and a small late Georgian hall beside it on the green hillside, falling steeply to the Eye Brook and looking across the frontier to the wooded hillside of Rutland, where it climbs skywards to Uppingham. Beautiful country at any time of the year. The church (St Peter) is mostly late 13th century (cf. the arcades) but thoroughly renewed 200 years later (Perpendicular windows especially). Some bench-ends of this date, and some glass also in the north aisle. Some medieval brasses, and an incised slab to Elizabeth Havers, 1634. A nice, lonely, atmospheric country church.

STOCKERSTON

STOKE GOLDING

Should be seen perhaps with Hallaton and Horninghold: a beautiful trio for a summer afternoon and evening, ending with dinner in the little hill-town of Uppingham (see *Shell Guide to Rutland*).

Stoke Golding (7) possesses one of the best village churches in the Midlands (St Margaret). A tablet in the north wall of the nave tells us it was built by Sir Robert de Campania and Margaret his wife in honour of St Margaret in the time of Edward I (1272–1307). The church is almost entirely of this period and although not large its arcades would do credit to a cathedral in their beauty. This is a church worth going many miles to see. Just outside the village to the west, on the north side of the minor road leading to Fenny Drayton, is Crown Hill. On this hillock, still almost in its natural state, occurred the memorable scene in which Sir William Stanley placed upon the head of Henry Earl of Richmond the crown of Richard III who had been killed at the battle of Bosworth Field earlier in the day. This small piece of ground looks as though it has not changed one scrap since that historic day in August 1485.

Stonesby (6) has a number of pleasant stone-built houses, as it stands on an outcrop of the Lincolnshire limestone. Running due south-east out of the village, past Stonesby Lodge, is an old drovers' road, formerly called Street Lane, which makes beautiful walking and picnic country as no cars can traverse it. The church (St Peter) is mostly Early English with Perpendicular tower of white limestone, rather like a Somerset tower. North arcade late 13th century, south arcade a little later. 12th-century font and some medieval benches.

Stoney Stanton (7). A large ugly village with quarries of a hard road stone that have been long worked. The church (St Michael) has been heavily Victorianised and the only feature of interest today is the Norman tympanum over the north

STONESBY

Slate detail in
SWITHLAND churchyard

doorway to the chancel. Pevsner calls this "a very odd representation" and asks "what is the meaning of this Germanic barbarity?"

Stonton Wyville (9), a small village in nice country but the church (St Denis) is a sad little place. It was mainly a 13th-century church but horribly over-restored in the Victorian period. It formerly had a south aisle of *c.* 1200, now blocked up. Only the Brudenell monuments are worth looking at, best of them being an alabaster tomb with a fine effigy of Edmund Brudenell, squire of Stonton, who died 12 May 1590. The Brudenells came here in Henry VIII's time and still own the manor. There are a number of later Brudenell memorials also, and in the small village some good stone-built houses, mainly 17th to 18th century.

Stoughton (5) was formerly "a pleasant scattered village", and even today has not suffered much from the proximity of Leicester. It is still surrounded by attractive open country. The church (St Mary and All Saints) has a large, rather bare interior with a 14th-century tower and a slender crocketed spire. The manor belonged to Leicester Abbey from the 12th century onwards and was one of its most important granges. After the Dissolution it was sold to the Farnhams of Quorndon, and in the church is an alabaster monument to George Farnham (d. 1562) and his wife. There is also a tablet to Sir Thomas Beaumont of Stoughton (d. 1614) and his wife and their ten children. There used to be a large house called Stoughton Grange, a Victorian version of the Elizabethan style, which was demolished in 1925–6. All that remains to show its former importance is a small lodge on the Gartree Road of *c.* 1820.

Stretton-en-le-Field (1) was formerly in Derbyshire and was transferred to Leicestershire in 1897. It consists of little more than the church and hall in a small park. The church (St Michael) is mostly 14th century in date, built of the local grey sandstone, with the usual Perpendicular changes. The font is unusual in date (about 1662). The hall was described

40 years ago as "an ancient mansion . . . surrounded by a shrubbery".

Sutton Cheney (7) has a very pleasant church (St James), light and well-cared for. It stands by itself on rising ground with a massive squat tower of 14th-century date and a top stage of early brickwork. The south aisle is early 14th century with good window tracery of the period. The Decorated church was restored in the early 19th century, a good period, and one sees traces of this. The whole church is plastered and whitened with much clear glass, and is to be commended to the ardent church-crawler.

A nice little row of almshouses lies to the east of the church with an inscription saying they were "repaired" in 1811. At the end of the village is a large 17th-century mansion. Just outside the village, in the fork of the road leading to Market Bosworth, is a well-defined *tumulus* which may well be the mound on which Richard III stood on the eve of Bosworth Field to speak to his troops. The battle of Bosworth Field, one of the great turning points in English history, was actually fought in the parish of Sutton Cheney, mostly along the ridge of high ground running south-west from the village and known as Ambion Hill. Richard's armies were drawn up along this ridge on the fatal day. Near Ambion Hill Farm is King Richard's Well, covering the spring at which he drank during the battle, but access to this historic hill is totally discouraged by the farmer, and visitors are far from welcome. Though the historic battle was fought in this parish, it was named after the little town of Market Bosworth which lies on the skyline to the north as being a better known landmark.

Sutton in the Elms (7), a most attractive name but not a very attractive village. It is, however, worth visiting to see the Baptist Chapel founded in 1650. Little or nothing remains of this building. The present building was repaired and enlarged about 1816 and this is basically what it feels like today inside, though somewhat Victorianised. In the chapel burial ground are some excellent

Swithland slate headstones of the best period—i.e. 18th century and early 19th—with beautiful lettering. Note especially one to a pastor who died in 1807.

Swannington (4) is a large village in the Leicestershire coalfield. Coal has been mined here since the 13th century, but Swannington is not a place to visit for pleasure, except perhaps for the industrial archaeologist. Here he will see a railway bridge built by Robert Stephenson and the remains of the incline on the Leicester to Swannington railway of 1832. The church (St George) was built in 1828 with a chancel added in 1900.

Swepstone (4) has the usual "Leicestershire period" church (St Peter), i.e. early 14th century with Perpendicular clerestory. Tower rebuilt *c.* 1840, chancel 1869.

Swinford (8). The church (All Saints) is 13th and 14th century in date, with a Norman font. East end of chancel rebuilt 1778 and remodelled in 1895.

Swithland (5) is one of the best known of the "Forest villages". Long famous for its slate quarries which produced roofing material from Roman times onwards. They finally ceased work in the late 19th century. The slate was widely used also for headstones in churchyards, those of the 18th century and early 19th being often beautiful examples of lettering and design. The church (St Leonard) is mostly 13th century, with a south aisle rebuilt in 1727. Fine slate wall monument *c.* 1750—"a *tour de force* of the slate workers" (Pevsner). Many fine headstones in churchyard, including one as early as 1673. Swithland Hall, 1834.

Sysonby (5) a hamlet one mile west of Melton Mowbray. The little church (dedication unknown) is built of local ironstone with a 13th-century saddle-backed tower, so common in this district. One sees the type at Welby, Wartnaby, and Brentingby also. The church, as usual, has been too much restored. Sysonby was formerly a village, and is one of the numerous depopulated villages of Leicestershire. It probably stood in the field to the west of the road leading down to the church where the line of the main street is plainly visible.

Syston (5) another large and ugly industrial village in the Soar valley, fog in winter and hot red-brick in summer. In the old village are some early examples of brick vernacular building (e.g. Brook Street, 1686). The large church (St Peter and St Paul) was much renewed in the 1870s. Good tower, Early English below, Perpendicular above; good nave roof, also Perpendicular. Panelled hexagonal piers and arches to the arcade.

Theddingworth (8) in the 1840s had a small cottage industry weaving silk plush for covering hats. The Grand Union Canal traverses the parish, about a mile away to the north, and

makes good walking for miles along the towpath, particularly eastwards beneath the picturesque Laughton Hills as far as Foxton locks, *q.v.*

The church (All Saints) is of considerable interest, especially for its good late Norman north arcade, *c.* 1190–1200 in date. The south arcade is a little later, *c.* 1220. Font *c.* 1200. Apart from this, the fabric is the usual late 13th–early 14th century, with Perpendicular windows and tower. There is a fine monument by Richard Hayward to the Rev. Slaughter Clarke. Some other minor monuments.

Thornton (4) is a long, ugly, one-street village on the edge of the Leicestershire coalfield, redeemed by the lake-like reservoir and the wooded hills of Charnwood behind, and by the exceptionally interesting church (St Peter). This again is the usual Leicestershire mixture of

Decorated and Perpendicular work. The main part of the fabric is *c.* 1300, but about 1500 the tower and spire were rebuilt, the clerestory added to the nave, a new font and screen put in, and a complete set of bench-ends, which miraculously survive. The remains of the screen retain their original colouring.

The whole interior is remarkable as an example of an unrestored medieval church with most of its original fittings. Besides those already mentioned, there are traces of medieval wall-painting, some early 14th-century stained glass in the south aisle, a maze in the floor of the nave, and a massive south door of early 14th-century date, said to have been brought from Ulverscroft priory. Note also the Italian painting over the altar, and the tympanum of 1820 over the chancel arch.

Thorpe Arnold (6) lies just outside

TWYCROSS

Melton Mowbray. Its ironstone church (St Mary) is mostly about 1300 in date, with a Perpendicular clerestory. A 12th-century font survives, however, from an earlier building. The church is attractively sited on a hilltop and was thoroughly restored in 1876.

Thorpe Langton (9) lies in a very unspoilt countryside, one of the several Langtons, as they are always called. The church (St Leonard) has a dumpy limestone broach spire and a bold west tower, all 13th century. The whole building, in fact, is late 13th century to early 14th century, though the south aisle might have

been rebuilt in the 17th century when other work was done to the fabric. The old village, now gone, stood close to the church. The Baker's Arms is a nice building of about 1720.

Thorpe Satchville (6), just outside Melton Mowbray, has been a well-known centre for hunting for several generations. Thorpe Trussels is a noted fox-cover in the parish beside the by-road to Kirby Gate. It was originally given to the poor as a cow-pasture many years ago and was later let to the Quorn as a cover. J. B. Firth, in the old *Highways and Byways in Leicestershire*, wrote about

1920 that "A large hunting stables adorns the entrance to the village on the Twyford side, and international finance, biscuits and whisky afford Thorpe Satchville's reputation for opulence. . . . Wealth abounding is not necessarily grace abounding. . . ." He also records that Mrs Hillyard, the lady champion of England at lawn tennis at various dates between 1886 and 1900, lived at Thorpe Satchville.

The hall is described by White in 1846 as "A neat cemented mansion with pleasant grounds", and this is still an adequate description. The church (St Michael) is mainly of ironstone with a nave and chancel

Cottage near ULVERSCROFT

in one, and a nice Swithland slate roof. It looks late Perpendicular, possibly even early 17th century, with Victorian changes. It has in fact, a pleasant, neat Victorian interior, all of 1861, and it stands unfenced on the village green well away from the main road.

Thringstone (4) is a long, unprepossessing village in the Leicestershire coalfield with a church (St Andrew) entirely built in 1863.

Thrussington (5), in the Wreak valley, is chiefly notable as the birthplace of John Ferneley in 1782, son of a wheelwright, whose animal and hunting pictures now command increasingly high prices. Most of his work was done at Melton Mowbray (*q.v.*). The church (Holy Trinity) is of ironstone and of no great interest. Mostly the "typical" Leicestershire period of late 13th–early 14th century, with a thin Perpendicular tower and clerestory of same date: all pretty heavily "restored" in 1877–88. The village has some good vernacular building.

Thurcaston (5) was the birthplace of Hugh Latimer (1470) whose father was a yeoman here. But the house now called Latimer's House is not the birthplace. This was pulled down years ago; the house now so described was built in 1568.

The church (All Saints) has a Norman south doorway. Tower *c*. 1200, with the usual Perpendicular top stage. Rest of church mostly late 13th century with Perpendicular changes (e.g. windows, south porch, and best of all the nave roof). Screen in north aisle may be as early as 1300. Screen under the tower, 15th century. A few minor monuments, the slate headstone to Elias Travers (1641) being the earliest in Leicestershire.

Thurlaston (7) church (All Saints) is mostly 13th century with some 15th-century additions, but the whole has been terribly over-restored (1850). In the north aisle are monuments of the Turvilles, ranging from 1340–1653. They lived at a place called New Hall, a moated site in the parish of which only a few fragments now remain.

Thurmaston (5) is yet another of the villages which has been totally engulfed by Leicester. There was a vigorous restoration of the church (St Michael) in 1848, except for the Perpendicular tower, but the north and south arcades date from *c*. 1300. Some years ago, in building a modern housing estate, a very large pagan cemetery of the earliest Anglo-Saxon period was found, probably dating from as far back as the late 5th century. If this is so, the cemetery may be an important link between Roman Britain and the Old English period.

Thurnby (5) was once a pleasant little village but is now well within the subtopian orbit of Leicester. The church (St Luke) probably stands on an ancient site, as four tombstones of 10th-century date were found during alterations to the Norman structure. Only one similar set of such tombstones is known. The Thurnby stones are now exhibited in the Jewry Wall Museum in Leicester. The present church has a central tower of which the lower part dates from the 12th century, then another stage of Early English, and finally a Decorated stage. The rest of the church is mostly early 14th century, much rebuilt 1870–73, with an Early English tub font.

Bushby, a hamlet of Thurnby, has no church of its own, and is rapidly becoming suburbanised like Thurnby.

Tilton on the Hill (6) stands on the top of the marlstone or ironstone escarpment which marks the edge of High Leicestershire. Seven hundred feet above sea-level, it is the highest village in the county, with beautiful views in all directions, especially eastwards over the wooded landscapes round Loddington, Launde, and Withcote.

The church (St Peter) is of the greatest rustic charm and architectural interest: built of a weather-beaten decaying ironstone with a slender limestone steeple. The 15th-century clerestory strikes one immediately with its tall, handsome windows. The older parts of the church are late 12th century—the tower arch, lower part of the tower, the font, and the priest's doorway. Most of the Norman church was

rebuilt between 1250 and 1350. Particularly good is the south aisle. The Decorated chancel (as witness the sedilia) was remodelled in the Perpendicular style, when the lofty clerestory was also added. Georgian communion rails. Digby monuments in the south aisle, which probably owes its scale to that eminent medieval family: Sir John Digby (1269) and wife, two recumbent effigies; and the tomb-chest of Sir Everard Digby (1509), with some lesser monuments of Elizabethan and Stuart date. The Digbys were here as early as 1234.

Tilton church never fails to appeal with its rural simplicity and clear light. One goes there again and again for sustenance, to feel "the secret influence of antiquity in stone-work, inscriptions, and inherited things. . . ."

Tugby (9) church (St Thomas à Becket) has a remarkable pre-Conquest tower, though the upper part may be just after 1066. Other Norman work in chancel wall, and south doorway. Otherwise, the main building is *c*. 1300 with Perpendicular clerestory. Beautiful Elizabethan monument to Richard Neeld, 1574. Also one to Thomas Wilson of Keythorpe Hall, 1720–30.

Tur Langton (8) is one of the numerous villages in the Langton district. The church (St Andrew) was rebuilt on a new site in 1866 in a hard red-brick, more suited to the suburb of some large industrial town. No doubt it will be admired in a hundred years' time as a specimen of its age. There are small remains of the old church at the west end of the village, near the 17th-century manor house.

Twycross (1) church (St James) is mostly Decorated in style. The great thing to see here is the medieval stained-glass in the east window, "of which much is of the finest quality available in the whole of Europe" (Pevsner). It was originally in various places in France: the centre light came from the Lady Chapel of St Denis in Paris. Some came from the Sainte-Chapelle, some from Le Mans cathedral, and some from St Julien-du-Sault. All presented to William IV, who in turn gave it to Earl Howe of Gopsall. He then presented it to his parish church at Twycross.

Twyford (5), set in peaceful undulating hunting country, has one outstanding feature in its church (St Andrew)—the north arcade of *c.* 1185, undoubtedly built by the masons who built the Castle Hall at Oakham, not so far away. Magnificent capitals to the piers. Much of the usual 15th-century work, e.g. the tower, and the nave windows. Pleasant village.

Ullesthorpe (7) is a large village in the parish of Claybrook (*q.v.*) so it has no Anglican church of its own. The older part of the village is away from the main road and contains a large and not unhandsome chapel (now Congregational) built in 1825. Framework-knitting used to be carried on here on a considerable scale.

Ulverscroft (4), in the midst of Charnwood Forest, was chosen as the site of an Augustinian priory by Robert Bossu, Earl of Leicester, in 1134. It is the largest monastic ruin in the county, which is not saying much. Most conspicuous is the 15th-century west tower: some of the fragmentary monastic buildings are 13th century. Visitors are not much encouraged. The priory was dissolved in 1539, and the site sold to the Earl of Rutland, a great receiver of monastic spoils in this part of England.

Waltham-on-the-Wolds (6) stands high on the oolitic limestone which crops out here, so that the village has many decent stone-built houses, more reminiscent of Lincolnshire than Leicestershire. The church (St Mary Magdalene) stands high with fine views to the north over the vale of Belvoir, a handsome church with a central tower. It is mainly a rebuilding of about 1300 with 15th-century alterations. It has a Norman font and an over-restored Norman south doorway. The north doorway is about 1200 in date.

In an early 19th-century Guide, Waltham is described as "a small market-town, situated in a hilly, barren, heathy tract". The market ended over 100 years ago, but there used also to be a great annual fair for horses and cattle. The village was

noted for shows of its Agricultural Association which had its own handsome Agricultural Hall built in the Tudor style in 1838.

Walton-on-the-Wolds (5) is described by Nichols as "a small village in a healthy air". The church was rebuilt in 1739 in brick, but of this church (St Mary) only the west tower survives, and the remainder is Victorian and very dull.

Wanlip (5) once stood alone near the Soar and well away from the A.6 but is now becoming part of the Greater Leicester sprawl. The very name showed its isolation—Old English *anliepe*, which means "isolated". The church (St Nicholas) has a 13th-century tower. It seems to have been rebuilt, according to the inscription on the medieval brass to Sir Thomas Walsh (d. 1393) and wife, which tells us that she "made the Kirke of Anlep", so it is now basically a late 14th-century church. There are good Perpendicular windows of this period on the south side of the chancel. Incidentally, the inscription on the Walsh brass is the first inscription in English on any brass.

Wartnaby (5). A tiny place, lost among the north Leicestershire wolds, which rise to 560 ft. north-east of the village. The first element in the name is probably from the Old English "watch-hill", a look-out post which commanded tremendous views northwards over the Trent valley as far as Lincoln minster. At Wartnaby Hall, Charles II "took breakfast with Mr Hacket, the then owner" while on a royal progress. Tower Cottage, south of the church, is dated 1656 above the front door, but the rear of the house has substantial remains of a 12th- or 13th-century building, possibly connected with the Knights Templar.

The church (St Michael) is called by Pevsner "an impressive and important church". The saddleback west tower (13th century) is another example of a local type, as at Welby, Sysonby, Brentingby, and elsewhere. Exterior much restored, but the blocked north doorway of *c.* 1200–20 suggests the date of the south arcade, of which the arches retain much original painting. Font also *c.* 1200. Some medieval benches.

Welby (5) is scarcely even a hamlet, two miles north-west of Melton Mowbray, and indeed is the site of a lost village which stood in the field immediately north and north-east of the church where a rectangular pattern, showing the old house sites, is plainly visible. There are also medieval fish-ponds by the stream on the east of the village site. The church (dedication appears to be unknown) has the usual small saddlebacked west tower of the district, probably 13th century. The rest of the church was rebuilt in the Perpendicular style and over-restored later. The interior is of no interest, except for a Jacobean reading-desk. In the 17th century a great house stood here: the Hearth Tax of 1664 shows that Dame Elizabeth Bennett then had a house with 24 hearths, but where this house stood is not very evident today.

Welham (9) is a tiny village beside the River Welland, here the county boundary with Northamptonshire. The church (St Andrew) stands alone near the river. It has a bold west Perpendicular tower and a generally 15th-century interior, but dull. The chancel is Victorian. In the north transept is an obelisk to Francis Edwards (1728).

The bridge over the Welland is the third on the site, the first being a private bridge erected in 1678. A footpath leads up to Langton Caudle, a prominent hill over 450 ft. high, from which there are beautiful views up and down the Welland Valley.

The original medieval village probably lay to the south of the church, which helps to explain the apparently isolated position of the building today. There was much rebuilding of the present village by Francis Edwards about 1720, of which the Old Red Lion is the best survival.

West Langton (8) has no church and no village, only Langton Hall in a small park. The hall was built in the early 17th century by Thomas Staveley (d. 1631), but later alterations have obscured this. The south wing was built in the 1660s with consider-

Georgian farm enclosure at WALTHAM-ON-THE-WOLDS

able alterations in the medieval style in 1802. Thomas Staveley the antiquary (d. 1684) was born here in 1626; and Hugo Meynell hunted the Quorn from here in the 1770s.

Whatborough (6) is the name of the highest hill (755 ft.) in east Leicestershire. On the flat top of this hill there was formerly a village which was depopulated about 1495. It had a church dedicated to St Nicholas, but all one can see today are the characteristic traces of an abandoned village. It was already decayed long before it was finally abandoned, possibly because of its extraordinary windswept position on the summit of a high hill, which suggests it was a very early settlement. From the top of the hill one gets fine views of the unexpectedly beautiful rolling country of east Leicestershire.

Whetstone (8) is a large and unattractive village too close to Leicester. As Pevsner says the church (St Peter) is mostly early 14th century; in fact there is a date 1335 cut on a buttress on the north side of the church door which probably represents the completion of the building. The church underwent the usual thorough restoration in which the tower and spire were entirely rebuilt in 1856, but the interior contains a good deal of work of the 1330s despite what the Victorians did to it.

Whitwick (4) is an elongated, unprepossessing mining village, but immediately to the north-east is some of the best Charnwood scenery, e.g. High Sharpley and Blackbrook Reservoir. As early as 1293 it had a weekly market and a four-day fair.

The church (St John the Baptist) has a bold Decorated tower. The rest of the church is also Decorated but over-restored. The much defaced alabaster effigy of a knight is that of Sir John Talbot of Swannington, early 15th century.

Mount St Bernard Abbey lies 1½ miles east of Whitwick. It was founded in 1835, the first Catholic abbey to be built in England since the Reformation for Cistercian monks, who chose their customary wild site. The buildings are mainly by Pugin (1839–44). The church was begun in 1843 and enlarged in 1934–9. The stalls in the church were designed by Eric Gill. The abbey church is an impressive building and worth while visiting.

Wigston Magna (8) has been engulfed in Leicester within the last 20 years

18th-century field pattern, WIGSTON MAGNA

and lost nearly all its village character: now it is, like Oadby, neither town nor village. It has two churches with steeples—hence its former name of Wigston Two Steeples. The parish church (All Saints) is large, mostly 1280–1330 but over-restored in 19th century. Handsome tower and spire, seen from miles away to the south. Nave roof 1637, alabaster Georgian font 1781.

The other church (St Wistan) was originally built *c.* 1280–1300, but rebuilt, except the tower, in 1853.

There used to be some decent brick vernacular building near the parish church—perhaps still there, though one always fears the worst near a developing city like Leicester. Turn one's back for a month and something good disappears in rubble and dust in the path of what is laughingly called Progress.

Wigston Parva (7) is a delightful hamlet around a small green just off the roaring A.46. Facing the green is a good brick building of 1727 (Hall Farm) with projecting wings. Also facing the green is what must have been the manor house which appears to have a 16th-century plan. The tiny church (St Mary) consists of nave and chancel in one, with a

small western bell turret. The only feature of antiquarian interest is the Norman doorway in the north wall. I suspect the church as a whole was rebuilt after a long period of decay, but it was nicely done and could be taken for the original structure. The original medieval timbers of the roof remain, but otherwise it is a quiet Victorian interior. Key at the cottage nearby.

Willesley (4) consists of little but the church today. The hall has been pulled down. The church (St Thomas) dates generally from the first half of the 14th century with a west tower added in 1845. There are monuments to the Hastings and Abney families.

Willoughby Waterless (8), a small but interesting village in pleasant unspoilt country. The name should be "Water-leys", quite the opposite meaning to that implied by the Ordnance Survey version. The church (St Mary) is inexcusably padlocked. It seems to be of a typical Leicestershire period, i.e. 13th–14th century, with a Perpendicular nave roof, and a Norman font from an earlier church on the site. The church was over-restored in the 1870s, when the chancel was rebuilt.

The village is exceptionally rich in handsome houses—several of them dated—of the late 17th to early 19th century, some of them the large houses of wealthy graziers of the time. At the south end of the village is the Old Hall which seems to be substantially a Tudor building.

Wistow (8), an attractive little church in a beautiful park which is much frequented at week-ends. The old village has disappeared. The hall is basically Jacobean, much altered about 1810. It was for long the residence of the Halfords, who bought the manor in 1603. Sir Richard Halford sheltered Charles I here after his crushing defeat at Naseby, 1645. Here also lived Sir Henry Halford, physician to George III, George IV, William IV, and Queen Victoria.

The church is dedicated to St Wistan, a Mercian royal prince who was almost certainly martyred here in the year 849 and afterwards canonised. Much of the fabric is Norman, though the tower was rebuilt in the late 15th century, and the nave, chancel, and north transept were extensively remodelled in 1746 (hence the large windows of clear glass) so that the general feeling of the church is Georgian. Complete furnishings of the period—box-pews, pulpit, reredos. Superb ironwork of communion rails, early 18th century. Several Halford monuments.

Withcote (6), set in beautiful hilly and wooded country, consists, like so many places in Leicestershire, of only the hall and the church. The village was depopulated in early Tudor times for sheep and cattle pastures. The hall was rebuilt in the early 18th century and is most appealing. Near it is the church, really a private chapel like that at Noseley, built 1500–10. Externally a Gothic building but internally a perfect 18th-century period piece arranged like a college chapel. It is of outstanding interest in every detail.

Witherley (1) was once a pleasant little village beside the River Anker, but is now heavily commuterised. The church (St Peter) stands attractively on the banks of the river, which it graces with its tall Perpendicular tower and spire. The nave and north aisle are early Decorated work with very good window tracery, but the chancel was rebuilt in 1858 in a hard way. The background to this pleasant scene is a steady thunderous noise from the A.5, one of the most loathsome roads in England as it strives to cross the west Midlands. Although it has the distinction of being the Roman Watling Street, no sane motorist should go near it, with its unceasing flood of heavy lorries which it is impossible to escape. There are a few nice houses in the

older part of Witherley, the most interesting being a yeoman's house of about 1600 just as one leaves the village on the road to Sheepy.

Woodhouse (4) started as a forest settlement in the 12th century. The name means "houses in the wood" and is self-explanatory. The village lies on the northern fringe of Charnwood Forest and is a favourite venue for week-end motorists. The church (St Mary) is of mixed dates with much 17th-century repair work and a pulpit dated 1615. It was, however, "thoroughly restored in 1878". Leicestershire churches seem to have suffered more than most from well-meaning "restorers", probably because it was in the 19th century a county of large estates and rich

WISTOW HALL

WISTOW

landlords with plenty of money to spend on doing up their local church. One wishes sometimes that there had been more poor landlords and less interference.

Woodhouse Eaves (4) one mile south-west, is now very much built up amid picturesque rocky scenery, especially at Hanging Stone Hills. Many of the older cottages are built of Forest stone with Swithland slate roofs. The church (St Paul) was built in 1837 by Railton and enlarged in 1880 by Christian. It stands in a fine position on the edge of an old slate quarry. At The Brand (private) are a number of disused slate pits. This slate, called Swithland slate after the village where it was mostly quarried, was used as far back as Roman times and continuously since the 13th century until the introduction of cheap Welsh

slates with the coming of canals and railways.

Beacon Hill is an Iron Age earthwork, rising to some 800 ft. above sea-level and commanding fine views of the Forest, especially northwards and eastwards.

Worthington (4). The church (St Matthew) lies alongside the road, long and narrow, with a continuous nave and chancel and a little western bell-cote. It seems to be 13th century throughout (note the single lancet windows) with a brick south porch of the 18th century and a bit of brick rebuilding at the east end of the chancel. I see no signs that it is a Norman church, as Pevsner says.

As one approaches Worthington from the south, notice the bold mass of Breedon Hill crowned by the equally bold church, like a miniature

Durham at a distance and obviously a very ancient site (*see* under Breedon-on-the-Hill).

Wyfordby (6), a tiny village with an ironstone church in the upper valley of the Eye—peaceful country all around, quite unlike what strangers associate with the East Midlands. The church (St Mary) is pleasant to look at from the outside—a 13th-century tower with a Perpendicular top stage, but the interior of about 1300 underwent the usual vigorous Victorian restoration and is of little interest. There is a considerable moated homestead immediately west of the church where the medieval lords of the manor of Wyfordby lived.

WISTOW

114

Wymeswold (5) is a large village which once had a weekly market, granted in 1338, and a yearly fair on the eve and feast of St Peter and St Paul, which may have been an earlier dedication of the parish church, now reputed to be dedicated to St Mary. Village fairs were usually held round about the dedication day of the church, which suggests that in this case, as in so many others, the dedication may have been changed subsequently. The market and fair were probably held on a small open space south-west of the church called The Stockwell.

The church has a handsome Perpendicular west tower, but the rest of it was restored by Pugin in 1844–5 when the north and south aisles were wholly rebuilt. This was in the time of Henry Alford, vicar 1835–53, who was afterwards Dean of Canterbury and the first editor of the *Contemporary Review*. It has a very attractive Victorian interior, whitened throughout, with coloured corbels to Pugin's nave roof. The furnishings are all by Pugin (font, pulpit, etc.) and all well-kept—this is one of the most attractive churches in the diocese.

There are many good houses in the village of 18th-century and early 19th-century date, and outside the village to the east are two good examples of old drovers' roads with exceptionally wide grass verges.

Wymondham (6) is a large pleasant village almost on the borders of Rutland. In its wide main street were held for centuries the weekly market and the annual fair granted as long ago as 1303. It was once a much larger place and the back lanes are probably decayed streets with old walls, old orchards, ironstone cottages, and farmhouses complete with white doves. There was probably a Roman villa here adjoining the present Wymondham House, as rather more than a century ago a considerable area of Roman pavement was discovered and other Roman remains have been found in the Rectory grounds.

The church (St Peter), on the southern edge of the village, is

WITHCOTE church

15th-century glass
at WITHCOTE

WITHCOTE Hall

mostly of ironstone, with Perpendicular addition to the tower and the spire, which are of limestone. Inside, unusual arcades with two carved early 14th-century capitals and a late 13th-century chancel with a fine east window. There are monuments to the Berkeleys, who owned the manor from the late 15th century onwards and sold it in 1630.

The Free School, a stone building adjoining the churchyard, was built in 1637 and still stands. It was built as a grammar school, later abandoned, and in 1885 renovated and opened as a reading-room.

118

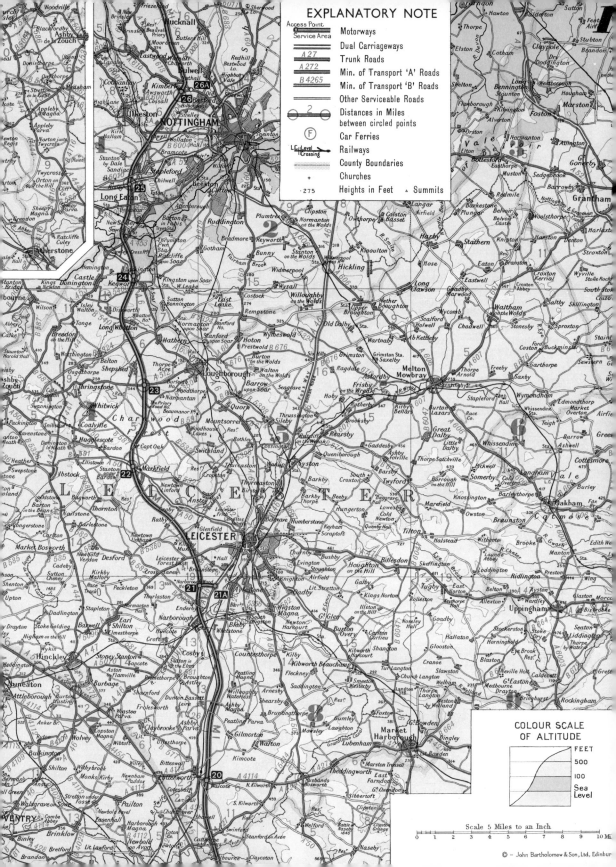

© – John Bartholomew & Son, Ltd, Edinbur

Index

Abbe family, *see* Ab Kettleby
Abney family, *see* Willesley
Adelaide, Queen, *see* Sibson
Aethelbald, King, *see* Gumley
Agricultural Association, *see* Waltham on-the-Wolds
Alford, Henry, *see* Wymeswold
Ambion Hill, *see* pp. 22, 23, Stapleton and Sutton Cheney
Ambion Wood, *see* p. 23
Anatomy of Melancholy, The, see Lindley
Ancient Kings Mills, The, see Castle Donington
Anglo Saxon remains, *see* Aylestone, Foston, Glen Parva, Harston, Leicester, Medbourne, Oadby, Saxby, Sproxton and Thurmaston
Anker, River, *see* Withcote
Ankle Hill, *see* Melton Mowbray
Anne of Cleves House, *see* Melton Mowbray
Anne, Queen, *see* Burrough-on-the-Hill and Little Dalby
Armston family, *see* Cosby
Art Gallery and Museum, *see* Leicester
Ascham, Roger, *see* Bradgate Park
Ashby family, *see* Aston Flamville, Hungerton and Lowesby
Ashby Pastures, *see* p. 16
Ashby, Shuckburgh, *see* Hungerton
Ashby-de-la-Zouch Canal, *see* Carlton, Congerstone, Dadlington and Shackerstone
Atherstone, *see* p. 22
Atherstone pack, *see* p. 16
Augustinians, *see* Breedon-on-the-Hill, Grace Dieu, Kirby Bellars, Launde, Owston and Ulverscroft
Avon, River, *see* Catthorpe and Stanford

Babington, Dr. Humphrey, *see* Barrow-upon-Soar
Bainbrigge family, *see* Lockington
Bakewell, Robert, *see* Dishley
Bale family, *see* Carlton Curlieu
"Banks, The", *see* Burton Overy
Banks, Thomas, *see* Hungerton
Bardon Hill, *see* p. 14
Basset family, *see* Sapcote
Baxtergate, *see* Loughborough
Beacon Hill, *see* Woodhouse Eaves
Beaconsfield, Lord and Lady, *see* Melton Mowbray
Beatty, Admiral Lord, *see* Brooksby and Melton Mowbray
Beaumanor family, *see* Beaumanor Park and Coleorton
Beaumont, John, *see* Grace Dieu
Beaumont, Sir Thomas, *see* Stoughton
Beler family, *see* Eye Kettleby
Beler, Lord Hamon, *see* Melton Mowbray
Belgrave family, *see* North Kilworth

Belvoir Castle, *see* Knipton and Redmile
Belvoir pack, *see* p. 16
Belvoir, Vale of *see* Barkestone, Belvoir, Branston, Harby, Hose, Long Clawson, Muston, Nether Broughton, Plungar, Waltham-on-the-Wolds
Benedictines, the, *see* Belvoir and Diseworth
Bennett, Dame Elizabeth, *see* Welby
Bennett, James Gordon, *see* Melton Mowbray
Bent, John, *see* Littlethorpe
Bent, William and Agnes, *see* Cosby
Berkeley family, *see* Wymondham
Betjeman, John, *see* p. 9
Beveridge, William, *see* Barrow-upon-Soar
Big Township Close, *see* Potters Marston
Billesdon Coplow, *see* p. 16
Bill's Hill, *see* Billesdon
Billson family, *see* Narborough
Black Death, *see* Brooksby, Burton Overy, Gaddesby, and Ratby
Blackbrook Reservoir, *see* Whitwick
Blackwood's Magazine, *see* Ashby-de-la-Zouch
Blomfield, *see* Loughborough and Prestwold
Bodley, *see* Leicester and South Kilworth
Boothby, Thomas, *see* p. 16
Bossu, Robert le, Earl of Leicester, *see* Groby and Ulverscroft
Bosworth Field, *see* pp. 22–23, Elmesthorpe, Lindley, Market Bosworth, Stoke Golding and Sutton Cheney
Boundy, Peter, *see* Edmondthorpe
Bracebridge, Samuel, *see* Fenny Drayton
Bradgate Park, *see* p. 14 and Newtown Linford
Bradgate, William, *see* Peatling Parva
Bradley, *see* Blaston
Bradshaws, The, *see* p. 22 and Stapleton
Brand, The, *see* Woodhouse Eaves
Brandon, *see* Little Dalby
Breedon Hill q.v. and Worthington
Breton, Richard, *see* Barwell
Brewer's Grave, *see* Harston
Bronze Age, *see* Beacon Hill and Harston
Brownlow, Jack, *see* p. 19
Brudenell family, *see* Cranoe and Glooston
Brudenell House, *see* Melton Mowbray
Brudenell monuments, *see* Stonton Wyville
Brudenell, Viscount, *see* Melton Mowbray
Bullen, Rev. Edward, *see* Eastwell
Bulwarks, The, *see* Breedon-on-the-Hill
Burdett, Sir Francis, *see* Kirby Bellars

Burnaby, Col. Fred, *see* Somerby Hall
Burne-Jones, *see* Sheepy Magna
Burns-Hartopp, *see* Little Dalby
Burton End, *see* Melton Mowbray
Burton Hill, *see* Melton Mowbray
Burton Lazars, *see* Melton Mowbray
Burton, Richard, *see* Lindley
Burton, William *see* Carlton Curlieu, Holyoak and Lindley
Bury Camp, *see* Ratby
Bushby, *see* Thurnby
Byron, Lord, *see* Kirkby Mallory

Caldwell, *see* Chadwell
Cambridge, Duke and Duchess of, *see* Melton Mowbray
Campania, Margaret and Sir Robert de, *see* Stoke Golding
canals, *see* Ashby-de-la-Zouch and Nottingham-Grantham
Canning, George, *see* Burbage
Cannock Chase, *see* Blackfordby
Cardigan, Lord, *see* Brooksby and Melton Mowbray
Carillon Tower, *see* Loughborough
Caroe, W. D., *see* Leicester
Castle Hall, Oakham, *see* Twyford
Castles, *see* Ashby-de-la-Zouch, Castle Donington, Groby, Hallaton, Hinckley, Leicester and Mountsorrel
Cave family, *see* Ingarsby
Cave, Dr. William, *see* Pickwell
Celtic Tau, see Copt Oak
Chaplain, W. A., *see* Melton Mowbray
Charles I, *see* Ashby-de-la-Zouch, Aylestone, Brooksby, Cotes, Kings Norton, Laughton and Wistow
Charles II, *see* Orton-on-the-Hill and Pickwell and Wartnaby
Charnwood Forest, *see* p. 12, Bagworth, Bardon Hill, Beacon Hill, Beaumanor Park, Blackfordby, Bradgate Park, Breedon-on-the-Hill, Carlton Curlieu, Copt Oak, Loughborough, Markfield, Quorndon, Rothley, Ulverscroft and Woodhouse
Charnwood stone, *see* Donington-le-Heath
cheese, *see* Leicestershire, Quenby and Stilton
Cheney, Col., *see* Gaddesby
Cheselden, William, *see* Burrough-on-the-Hill
Cheseldyne Farm, *see* Burrough-on-the-Hill
Cheshire Home, *see* Staunton Harold
Chessher, Dr. Robert, *see* Peckleton
Chester, Earl of, *see* Beaumanor Park
Christian, Dick, *see* Melton Mowbray
Christian, Ewan, *see* Belgrave, Nailstone and Woodhouse Eaves
Churchill, Sir Winston, *see* Melton Mowbray
Cistercians, *see* Garendon and Whitwick

Civil Wars, *see* Ashby-de-la-Zouch, Belvoir and Kirby Muxloe

Clapham, Sir Alfred, *see* Breedon-on-the-Hill

Clarke, Rev. Slaughter, *see* Theddingworth

Cleveland, Duke and Duchess of, *see* Melton Mowbray

Clock tower, *see* Leicester

Clovis, King, *see* Long Clawson

coal, *see* Ashby-de-la-Zouch, Bagworth, Coalville, Coleorton, Donington-le-Heath, Measham, Snibston, Swannington, Thornton, Thringstone and Whitwick

Coalville q.v. and p. 19

Cockerell, C. R., *see* Coleorton

Codyngton, Henry, *see* Bottesford

Cold Newton, *see* Lowesby

Cole, William, *see* Laughton

Coleridge, *see* Coleorton

Constable, *see* Coleorton

Constantine, Arch of, *see* Gopsall

Constantine the Great, *see* Gumley

Contemporary Review, *see* Wymeswold

Coritani, the, *see* Burrough-on-the-Hill and Leicester

Corn Exchange, *see* Leicester

Cooch Behar, Maharanee of, *see* Melton Mowbray

Cotes de Val, *see* Dunston Basset

Cottesmore pack, *see* p. 16

Coventry, Hon. H. A., *see* Melton Mowbray

Coventry House, *see* Melton Mowbray

Crabbe, George, *see* Muston

Craven Lodge, *see* Melton Mowbray

Craven, Hon. W., *see* Melton Mowbray

Crew, Nathaniel, *see* Newbold Verdon

Crimea, *see* Melton Mowbray

Croft Hill, *see* Huncote

Cromwell, Gregory, *see* Knossington and Launde

Cromwell, Oliver, *see* Prestwold

Cromwell, Thomas, *see* Knossington and Launde

Cropston reservoir, *see* Bradgate Park

Crowland Abbey, *see* Beeby

Crown Hill, *see* p. 23 and Stoke Golding

Crozier, Temple, *see* Coston

Culey family, *see* Ratcliffe Culey

Culloden, *see* Dunton Basset

Cumberland, Duke of, *see* Dunton Basset

Cunard family, *see* Nevill Holt

Daffy, Rev. Thomas, *see* Redmile

Dalby Hall, *see* Old Dalby

Dance, George, *see* Coleorton

Danelaw, *see* Melton Mowbray

Danes, the, *see* Breedon-on-the-Hill

Deacon family, *see* Nailstone

Description of Leicestershire, The, *see* Holyoak and Lindley

le Despencer, Hugh, *see* Arnesby

Devon valley, *see* Branston and Knipton

Digby family, *see* Tilton-on-the-Hill

Directory, *see* White's *Directory*

Dissolution, the, *see* Belton, Garendon, Knossington, Launde and Stoughton

Dixie, Rev. John and family, *see* Market Bosworth

Doddridge, Dr. Philip, *see* Kibworth

Domesday Book, *see* Castle Donington and Chadwell

Donington Hall, *see* Castle Donington

Donington Park, *see* Castle Donington

Dormer, Richard, *see* Market Harborough

Drift, the, *see* Buckminster and Sewstern

Dudley, Rev. John, *see* Humberstone

Dysart family, *see* Buckminster

earthworks, *see* Foston, Gilmorton, Glen Parva, Hallaton, Hamilton, Kirby Bellars, Ratby, Saltby and Woodhouse Eaves

Edward the Martyr, *see* Castle Donington

Edward I, *see* Stoke Golding

Edward III, *see* Misterton

Edward VI, *see* Ashby-de-la-Zouch

Edward VII, *see* Gopsall and Melton Mowbray

Edwards, Francis, *see* Welham

Edwin, King and Martyr, *see* Scalford

Egerton Lodge, *see* Melton Mowbray

Elgin Lodge, *see* Melton Mowbray

Englefield, Lady, *see* Shoby

Everard, Stephen, *see* Heather

Eye brook, *see* Allexton, Bescaby, Brentingby, Buckminster, Coston, Eye Kettleby, Garthorpe, Stockerston and Wyfordby

Eye brook reservoir, *see* Holyoak

fairs, *see* Arnesby, Belton, Billesdon, Kegworth, Loughborough, Shepshed, Mountsorrel, Packington, Waltham-on-the-Wolds and Wymeswold

Faithful, Mrs. Patty, *see* Eastwell

Fanshawe, John, *see* Cotesbach

Farnham family, *see* Quorndon and Stoughton

Faunt family, *see* Foston

Fenny Drayton q.v. and p. 23

Ferneley, John, *see* Melton Mowbray and Thrussington

Fernie Pack, *see* p. 16

Ferrers, Earl, *see* Ratcliffe-on-the-Wreak and Staunton Harold

Ferrey, Benjamin, *see* Barlestone

Firth, J. B., *see* Thorpe Satchville

Flamville family, *see* Aston Flamville

Fortreys, *see* Kings Norton

Fosse Way, *see* Claybrooke, Ratby and Seagrave

Fox, George, *see* Fenny Drayton

fox-hunting, *see* p. 16, Ashby Folville, Billesdon, Kirby Bellars, Melton Mowbray, Quorndon, Thorpe Satchville and Twyford

Foxton Locks, *see* Laughton

Freeman, Rev. Thomas, *see* Bruntingthorpe

Fuller, Thomas, *see* Carlton Curlieu

Garendon Abbey q.v. and Dishley and Shepshed

Garofalo, *see* Buckminster

Gartree Road, *see* Glooston, Great Stretton, Medbourne and Stoughton

George III, *see* Oadby

Gibbons, Grinling, *see* Bottesford

Gill, Eric, *see* Whitwick

Glen Hill, *see* Glen Parva

Goldsmith Grange, *see* Scalford

Goldsmith, John, *see* Scalford

Gracedieu Priory, *see* Belton

Grand Union Canal, *see* Aylestone, Blaby, Foxton, Kegworth, Kilby, Laughton, Mountsorrel, Newton Harcourt, North Kilworth, Saddington and Theddingworth

Grant, Sir Francis, *see* Melton Mowbray

Grantham Canal, *see* Nottingham-Grantham Canal

Great Meeting, *see* Leicester

Greene, Sir Henry, *see* Kegworth

Grey family, *see* Bradgate Park, Evington and Groby

Grosseteste, Bishop, *see* Market Harborough

Gumley hills, *see* Smeeton Westerby

Gumley Park, *see* Laughton

Guide to Ashby-de-la-Zouch, *see* Ashby-de-la-Zouch

Guide to the City of Leicester, *see* Belgrave

Hacket, Mr., *see* Wartnaby

Halford family, *see* Wistow

Hall Farm, *see* Castle Donington

Hall, Rev. Robert, *see* Arnesby

Hamilton Lodge, *see* Melton Mowbray

Hamilton, Lord, *see* Melton Mowbray

Hamwell Spring, *see* Bescaby

Hanbury family, *see* Church Langton

Hanbury Trust, *see* Church Langton

Handel, G. F., *see* Gopsall

Hanging Stone Hills, *see* Woodhouse Eaves

Hansom, J. A., *see* Leicester and Ratcliffe-on-the-Wreak

Harborough, Earl of, *see* Stapleford

Hardwick, John, *see* p. 23 and Lindley

Hartopp family, *see* Little Dalby

Hastings Chapel, *see* Ashby-de-la-Zouch

Hastings family, *see* Ashby-de-la-Zouch and Aston Flamville

Hastings House, *see* Loughborough

Hastings, Lady Flora, *see* Ashby-de-la-Zouch

Hastings, Marquess of, *see* Castle Donington and Melton Mowbray

Hastings monuments, *see* Willesley

Hastings, William Lord, *see* Kirby Muxloe

Hasylryg, Robert and Eleanor, *see* Castle Donington

Havers, Elizabeth, *see* Stockerston

Hayward, Richard, *see* Theddingworth

Hazlerigg family, *see* Noseley

hearth tax, *see* Cosby and Welby

Heathcott, William, *see* Aylestone

Heckadeck Cottage, *see* Nether Broughton

Henry II, *see* Market Harborough

Henry VII, *see* pp. 12, 22, Lindley; *see also* Richmond, Earl of

Henry VIII, p. 16, Coleorton, Cranoe, Grace Dieu, Launde, Misterton and Peatling Magna

Herrick family, *see* Beaumanor Park and Houghton-on-the-Hill

Hickson, Thomas, *see* Melton Mowbray

Highways and Byways in Leicester, see Thorpe Satchville

Hillyard, Mrs., *see* Thorpe Satchville

Hopton, Thomas, *see* Old Dalby

Hoskins, Rev. H. J., *see* Blaby

Hotoft, Richard, *see* Humberstone

Howe, Earl, *see* Congerstone, Gopsall and Twycross

Hudson, Robert, *see* Melton Mowbray

hunting park, *see* Bradgate Park

Huntingdon, Earl and Countess of, *see* Ashby-de-la-Zouch and Burton-on-the-Wolds

Iron age, *see* Breedon-on-the-Hill, Burrough-on-the-Hill and Harston

Iron ore, *see* Asfordby, Hallaton, Harston and Holwell

Ivanhoe Baths, *see* Ashby-de-la-Zouch

James I, *see* Ashby-de-la-Zouch, Brooksby and Kings Norton

"James's Powder", *see* Redmile

Jelly's Wharf, *see* Mountsorrel

Jennens, Charles and Humphrey, *see* Gopsall

Jervis family, *see* Peatling Magna

Jewry Wall museum, *see* Leicester and Thurnby

Johnson, Gerard, *see* Bottesford

Johnson, John, *see* Leicester

Johnson, Nicholas, *see* Bottesford

Kempe, *see* Little Dalby, Market Bosworth, Peckleton and Sheepy Magna

Kendall headstones, *see* Church Langton

Kent, William, *see* Ashby-de-la-Zouch

Ketton stone, *see* Church Langton, Loddington and Shangton

Key House, *see* Castle Donington

Keythorpe Hall, *see* Tugby

King Lud's Entrenchments, *see* Saltby

King Richard's Well, *see* p. 23 and Sutton Cheney

Kings Mills, *see* Castle Donington

Kirby Bellars q.v. and p. 19

Kirby Gate, *see* p. 16

Knaptoft q.v. and Mowsley

Knights Templars, *see* Rothley and Wartnaby

knitting, framework, *see* Dunton Basset, Fleckney, Hathern, Kegworth, Long Whatton, Markfield and Ullesthorpe

Langley Priory, *see* Diseworth

Langton Caudle, *see* Welham

Langton Hall, *see* West Langton

Latimer, Hugh, *see* Thurcaston

Latimer's House, *see* Thurcaston

Laud, Archbishop, *see* North Kilworth

Launde Priory, *see* Loddington

Lee, J. M., *see* Castle Donington

Leesthorpe, *see* Pickwell

Legra, see Leire

Leicester q.v. and p. 19

Leicester Abbey, *see* Hemington and Ingarsby

Leicester, Earls of, *see* Earl Shilton and Groby

Leicestershire and Rutland, see Garendon

Leicestershire cheese, *see* p. 19 and Aston Flamville

leper hospital, *see* Burton Lazars

Lilley, William, *see* Diseworth

limestone, *see* Barrow-upon-Soar

Lindridge, *see* Desford

Lisle, Ambrose de, *see* Grace Dieu

Little Dalby q.v. and p. 19

Little Guide, see Braunstone, Castle Donington, Evington, Long Clawson, Melton Mowbray, Ragdale and Saxelby

Lovelace, Ada Augusta, *see* Kirkby Mallory

Lubenham Lodge, *see* Laughton

Ludeca, see Saltby

Lutyens, *see* Leicester and Lowesby

Macaulay, Thomas Babington, *see* Rothley

Manduessedum, see Kirkby Mallory and Peckleton

Marefield, North, *see* Owston

Marefield, Old, *see* Owston

markets, open-air, *see* Arnesby, Belton, Billesdon, Kegworth, Loughborough, Market Bosworth, Melton Mowbray, Packington, Shepshed, Waltham-on-the-Wolds, and Wymeswold

Marlstone uplands, *see* Galby

Malvern Hills, *see* Bardon Hill

Manners family, *see* Belvoir

Markham, Charles, *see* Church Langton

Martin family, *see* Anstey

Mary, Queen of Scots, *see* Ashby-de-la-Zouch

Medenborough, see Medbourne

Mercia, King of, *see* Breedon-on-the-Hill

Melbourne, Lord, *see* Melton Mowbray

Melton Mowbray q.v. and p. 19

Melville, George Whyte, *see* Melton Mowbray

Meynell, Hugo, *see* p. 16, Quorndon and West Langton

Midland England, see p. 19

Miles, Richard, *see* Cosby

Moira Baths, *see* Ashby-de-la-Zouch

Moira Colliery, *see* Ashby-de-la-Zouch and Donisthorpe

Monk, Mr., *see* p. 19

Montagu, Lady Mary Wortley, *see* Newbold Verdon

de Montfort Hall, *see* Leicester

Moore, John, *see* Sibson

Moore, Sir John, *see* Appleby Parva

Mount St. Bernard Abbey, *see* Whitwick

Mowbray family, *see* Aston Flamville and Melton Mowbray

Munt Sorel, *see* Mountsorrel

Murray's *Handbook, see* Bardon Hill

museums, *see* Belgrave, Jewry Wall, Newarke Houses and Art Gallery and Museum

Naseby, *see* Wistow

National Coal Board, *see* Coleorton

Neale, Thomas, *see* Sibson

Needham, John, *see* Burton Overy

Needham monuments, *see* Illston-on-the-Hill

Neeld, Richard, *see* Tugby

Nether Hall, *see* Scraptoft

Nevill, Sir Thomas, *see* Nevill Holt

New Hall, *see* Thurlaston

New York Herald, see Melton Mowbray

Newarke, *see* Leicester

Newarke Houses museum, *see* Leicester

Newbold, *see* Owston

Nicholas, John, *see* p. 19, Aston Flamville, Burbage, Drayton, Keyham and Walton-on-the-Wolds

Nicolson, Harold, *see* Leicester

Noel family, *see* Kirkby Mallory and Old Dalby

Noel family monuments, *see* Kirkby Mallory

Nonconformists, *see* Leicester

Norfolk, Duke of, *see* p. 22

Norman Conquest, *see* Bringhurst and Carlton Curlieu

Nottingham-Grantham Canal, *see* Barkestone, Harby, Hose, Knipton and Redmile

November Fair, *see* Loughborough

Novelty Theatre, *see* Coston

Old Hayes, *see* Ratby

Old John, *see* Bradgate Park

Old Moore's Almanac, *see* Diseworth

Oppenheim, E. Phillips, *see* Evington

Ordish, *see* Leicester

Orton Hall, *see* Orton-on-the-Hill

Orton, Mrs., *see* p. 19 and Little Dalby

Overton, *see* Coleorton

Owston Abbey, *see* Knossington

Oxford and Asquith, Earl of, *see* Melton Mowbray

Packe family, *see* Cotes and Prestwold

Packe Hall, *see* Gaddesby

Paget family, *see* Humberstone

Palmer, Geoffrey, *see* Carlton Curlieu

Palmer, Sir John, *see* Carlton Curlieu

Palmer, Thomas, *see* Nevill Holt

Papworth, *see* Nevill Holt

Parker, Richard, *see* Bottesford

Parsons, William, *see* Leicester

Pearson, J. L., *see* Mowsley

Peck, Francis, *see* Goadby Marwood

Penny, Bishop, *see* Leicester

Perkins, Rev. D. Steele, *see* Orton-on-the-Hill

Perkins, Dr. Humphrey, *see* Barrow-upon-Soar
Perry-Herricks, *see* Beaumanor Park
Peter's Pence, *see* Church Langton
Peters, Williams, *see* Knipton
Pevsner, Nikolaus, *see* Ashby-de-la-Zouch, Belton, Belvoir, Bottesford, Breedon-on-the-Hill, Church Langton, Coalville, Cold Overton, Diseworth, Gaddesby, Garendon, Kings Norton, Launde, Leicester, Market Bosworth, Melton Mowbray, Newtown Linford, Old Dalby, Owston, Peckleton, Prestwold, Saxby, Shepshed, Stapleford, Staunton Harold, Stoney Stanton, Swithland, Twycross, Wartnaby, Whetstone, Worthington
Pochin family, *see* Barkby
Pope, Alexander, *see* Gopsall
pork pies, *see* p. 19 and Melton Mowbray
pottery, *see* Lowesby
Poultney family, *see* Misterton
Poultney, *see* Kimcote and Misterton
Powell, York, *see* Great Bowden
Phillipps family, *see* Shepshed
Phillipps, Sir Ambrose, *see* Garendon
Plymouth Lodge, *see* Melton Mowbray
Premonstratensians, *see* Croxton
Priory Farm, *see* Blaston and Shoby
Pugin, *see* Little Dalby, Melton Mowbray, Ratcliffe-on-the-Wreak, Shepshed, Whitwick and Wymeswold
Pulteney Bridge, *see* Misterton
Purefoy monuments, *see* Fenny Drayton
Pytchley pack, *see* p. 16

Quakers, *see* Fenny Drayton
Quenby cheese, *see* p. 19
Quorn Hunt, *see* p. 16, Kirby Bellars, Quorndon, Thorpe Satchville, and West Langton

Railton, *see* Woodhouse Eaves
railways, *see* Glenfield, Stapleford and Swannington
Ratae Coritanorum, see Burrough-on-the-Hill and Leicester
Richard III, *see* pp. 22–23, Elmesthorpe, Market Bosworth, Stapleton, Stoke Golding and Sutton Cheney
Richardson, George, *see* Saxby and Stapleford
Richardson, Sir Benjamin, *see* Somerby
Richmond, Earl of, *see* Lindley, Stapleton and Stoke Golding
Rise and Fall of a Market Town, see Castle Donington
Rockingham Castle, *see* Bringhurst and Drayton
Roman remains, *see* Kirby Bellars and Oadby
Roman times, *see* Leicester
Roman villas, *see* Glooston, Hamilton, Medbourne and Wymondham
Roos, Robert de, *see* Bottesford
Rouen glass, *see* Coleorton
Royal Academy, *see* Bruntingthorpe

Rutland, Earls of, *see* Croxton, Garendon and Muston; monuments of, *see* Bottesford; *see also* Manners family

saline springs, *see* Ashby-de-la-Zouch
Salvin, *see* Sewstern
Saunders family, *see* Shangton
Saunders, Laurence, *see* Church Langton
Saxon, *see* Anglo Saxon
Scarbrow, Elizabeth, *see* p. 19
Scott, Sir Gilbert, *see* Birstall and Loughborough
Scott, Sir Walter, *see* Coleorton
Sence, River, *see* Sheepy Magna
Seven Deserted Village Sites in Leicestershire, see Cold Newton
Severn river, *see* Dunton Basset
Sewstern Lane, *see* Buckminster, Coston, Harston and Sewstern
Simmons, Jack, *see* Belgrave, Humberstone and Leicester
Shenton q.v. and p. 23
Sherard, Thomas, *see* Stapleford
Shipley Hill, *see* Ratcliffe-on-the-Wreak
Shirley Chapel, *see* Breedon-on-the-Hill
Shirley family, *see* Staunton Harold
Shirley, Sir Henrey, *see* Ragdale
Shuttleworth, Henry, *see* Great Bowden
Simmons, Jack: *Guide to Leicester, see* Belgrave, Leicester
Skeffington monuments, *see* Skeffington
Skipwith family, *see* Cotes and Prestwold
Smirke, S., *see* Leicester
Smith family, *see* Ashby Folville
Smith monuments, *see* Edmondthorpe
Smith, Rt. Hon. John, *see* Frolesworth
Soar, River, *see* p. 9, Aylestone, Beacon Hill, Cossington, Enderby, Hathern, Kegworth, Knaptoft, Mountsorrel, Syston and Wanlip
Somerset, Dukes of, *see* Burton-on-the-Wolds
Sottesbrigge, *see* Hathern
Southey, *see* Coleorton
Squires, William, *see* Burton Lazars
Stanley family, *see* p. 23
Stanley, H. M., *see* Melton Mowbray
Stanley, Sir William, *see* Stoke Golding
Stapleton q.v. and p. 22
Staresmore, Francis, *see* Frolesworth
Staunton, Robert and Agnes, *see* Castle Donington
Staveley, Christopher, *see* Melton Mowbray
Staveley Lodge, *see* Melton Mowbray
Staveley, Thomas, *see* West Langton
Stephen, King, *see* Groby, Hallaton and Newbold Verdon
Stephenson, George, *see* Snibston
Stephenson, Robert, *see* Swannington
Stewarts and Lloyds, *see* Melton Mowbray
Stilton cheese, *see* p. 19, Little Dalby, Melton Mowbray and Old Dalby
Stirling and Gowan, *see* Leicester

Stoke Golding, *see* p. 23
Stoneygate, *see* Leicester
Street, G. E., *see* Blaston and Leicester
Street Lane, *see* Stonesby
Strozzi, Bernardo, *see* Saxelby
Swithland slate, *see* Burton Lazars, Church Langton, Cosby, Fleckney, Leicester, Lutterworth, Mountsorrel, Narborough, Osgathorpe, Rotherby, Rothley, Scraptoft, Sutton in the Elms, Swithland, Thorpe Satchville and Woodhouse Eaves
Swift, Dean, *see* Houghton-on-the-Hill
Swift, River, *see* Gilmorton, Lutterworth and Misterton
Sugarloaf mountain, *see* Bardon Hill
Sutton Cheney q.v., p. 22 and Stapleton
Sysonby Lodge, *see* Melton Mowbray

Talbot, Sir John, *see* Whitwick
Taylor family, *see* Loughborough
Teck, Princess May of, *see* Melton Mowbray
Teulon, S. S., *see* Leicester
Theddingworth Lodge, *see* Laughton
Thompson, Hamilton, *see* Lockington
Thoroton, Sir John, *see* Belvoir
Thorpe Trussels, *see* Thorpe Satchville
Throsby, Mr., *see* Knighton and Medbourne
Todeni, Robert de, *see* Belvoir
Tomb in the Church of Brou, The, see Edmondthorpe
Tomblin, Thomas, *see* Billesdon
Tooley Park, *see* p. 16
Tower Cottage, *see* Wartnaby
Travers, Elias, *see* Thurcaston
Trent, River, *see* p. 9, Beacon Hill, Breedon-on-the-Hill, Castle Donington, Dunton Basset, Harston, Knaptoft and Wartnaby
Turville family, *see* Aston Flamville and Thurlaston
Tweed, River, *see* p. 22
Tyrell, Sir Thomas, *see* Old Dalby

Ulverscroft priory, *see* Thornton
University of Technology, *see* Loughborough
Utber, Martha, *see* Barrow-upon-Soar

Vanderbilt family, *see* Melton Mowbray
Venonae, see Claybrooke
de Verdon, Bertram, *see* Newbold er-Verdon
de Verdun, Roesia, *see* Belton
Vergil, Polydore, *see* Church Langton
Vernon family, *see* Aylestone
Victoria, Queen, *see* Rolleston
Village, The, see Muston
Villiers family, *see* Brooksby and Goadby Marwood

Wales, Prince of (Edward VII), *see* Melton Mowbray
Walker, Robert, *see* Fleckney
Walsh, Sir Thomas, *see* Wanlip
Walters, F., *see* Ashby-de-la-Zouch
War Office, *see* Beaumanor Park

Waring, Sir Samuel, *see* Gopsall
Warwick, Countess of, *see* Melton Mowbray
Warwick Lodge, *see* Melton Mowbray
Waterford, Marquis of, *see* Melton Mowbray
Watling Street, *see* p. 22, Catthorpe, Claybrooke, Fenny Drayton, Lindley, Peckleton and Witherley
Welland valley, *see* Bringhurst, Drayton, Great Easton, Harston, Knaptoft, Market Harborough, Nevill Holt, and Welham
Wells, Edward, *see* Cotesbach
Westley, John, *see* Gopsall
Westmacott, *see* Lutterworth
Whalley family, *see* Kings Norton
Whatborough Hill, *see* p. 12
Whatton Hall, *see* Long Whatton
White Moors, *see* p. 23
White's *Directory*, *see* Ashby-de-la-Zouch, Bardon Hill, Copt Oak, Diseworth, Elmesthorpe, Kirkby Mallory, Lowesby, Medbourne, Melton Mowbray, Misterton and Somerby
Whitwick colliery, *see* Coalville

Whissendine Brook, *see* p. 16
Wightman, Richard, *see* Burbage
Wiglaf, King, *see* Croft
Wigley monuments, *see* Scraptoft
Wilkie, *see* Coleorton
William I, *see* Belvoir
William III, *see* Bradgate Park
William IV, *see* Twycross
Wilson, Thomas, *see* Tugby
Wilson, Sir William, *see* Appleby Parva
Wilton, Earl of, *see* Melton Mowbray
Wing, John the elder, *see* Galby
Wing, John the younger, *see* Kings Norton
Winstanley family, *see* Braunstone
Witham, River, *see* Buckminster
Wolds, *see* Ab Kettleby, Eastwell and Hose
Wolsey Limited, *see* Fleckney
Woodford, Miss, *see* Keyham
Woodford, Ralph, *see* Ashby Folville
Woodhouse Eaves, *see* Beacon Hill
Wollaston, Richard, *see* Lowesby
Woodyer, *see* Smeeton Westerby
Worcester, Marquis of, *see* Melton Mowbray

Wordsworth, *see* Coleorton
Works, Ministry of, *see* Kirby Muxloe
Wreak river and valley, *see* Asfordby, Bescaby, Brooksby, Eye Kettleby, Frisby-on-the-Wreak, Hoby, Kirby Bellars, Melton Mowbray, Ragdale, Ratcliffe-on-the-Wreak, Rotherby and Thrussington
Wren, Christopher, *see* Appleby Parva
Wright, Sir Nathan, *see* Brooksby
Wyatt, James, *see* Belvoir and Melton Mowbray
Wyattville, *see* Gopsall
Wycliffe, *see* Lutterworth
Wycombe, *see* Chadwell
Wyndham, Colonel, *see* Melton Mowbray
Wyndham Lodge, *see* Melton Mowbray

Young, Arthur, *see* Medbourne

Zborowski, Counts, *see* Burton Lazars and Melton Mowbray
Zouch Bridge, *see* Hathern
la Zouch family, *see* Ashby-de-la-Zouch